ORACLE OF THE ILLUMINATI

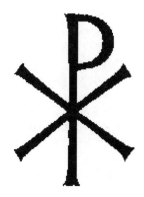

"IN THIS SIGN CREATE PEACE"

WILLIAM HENRY

Also by William Henry

CITY OF PEACE: THE HOLY GRAIL SECRETS OF ANCIENT
AND MODERN NASHVILLE

BLUE APPLES: A SEARCH FOR THE LOST STARGATE
ARTIFACTS AND SPIRITUAL TEACHINGS OF JESUS AND
MARY MAGDALENE

THE LANGUAGE OF THE BIRDS: OUR ANGELIC CONNECTION

THE A~TOMIC CHRIST: F.D.R.'S SEARCH FOR THE SECRET
TEMPLE OF THE CHRIST LIGHT

GOD MAKING: HOW ANCIENT MYTHS OF DNA REVEAL THE
MIRACLE HEALING POWER OF OUR MYSTIC ANATOMY

THE HEALING SUN CODE: REDISCOVERING THE SECRET
SCIENCE AND RELIGION OF THE GALACTIC CORE AND THE
REBIRTH OF EARTH IN 2012

THE CRYSTAL HALLS OF CHRIST'S COURT: NEW
REVELATIONS OF THE FORBIDDEN SECRETS OF ATLANTIS,
THE HOLY GRAIL AND THE INNER EARTH

ARK OF THE CHRISTOS: THE MYTHOLOGY, SYMBOLISM
AND PROPHECY OF THE RETURN OF PLANET X AND THE
AGE OF TERROR

CLOAK OF THE ILLUMINATI: SECRETS. TRANSFORMATIONS.
CROSSING THE STARGATE

Also visit his web site at

http://www.Williamhenry.net

ORACLE OF THE ILLUMINATI

CONTACT. CO-CREATION. COINCIDENCE.

WILLIAM HENRY

COVER BY DANA AUGUSTINE

SCALA DEI
Nashville

Oracle of the Illuminati

By William Henry

Copyright 2005 by William Henry

Published by
Adventures Unlimited Press
Kempton, Illinois 60946 USA

www.adventuresunlimitedpress.com
www.adventuresunlimited.nl

ISBN 1-931882-52-5

Printed on acid free paper in the United States of America

10 9 8 7 6 5 4 3 2 1

CONTENTS

1.

FROM *CLOAK* TO *ORACLE*

Since the 13ᵗʰ century invention of eyeglasses by an anonymous inventor in Italy there has existed the radical idea (and heretical, by Dark Age Church standards, which is why the inventor kept his idea quiet), that the human body is improvable. No longer were humans subject to the flaws of the maker or the oppressive control of a corrupt priesthood. Humans were free to choose or select for themselves improvements to their body and to 'polish the pearl', so to speak.

This was an inconvenient time to introduce such a heretical idea. The Church of Roma was hung-over from a horrific binge of killing during which as many as one million peaceful men, women and children who called themselves Cathars ("Pure Ones") had been gruesomely exterminated in the first European holocaust or ethnic cleansing. Dwelling in the patch of paradise that stretches from Northern Spain across the southern provinces of France, they claimed to be direct descendents of the early Gnostic Christians, many of who it is claimed fled to southern France to escape the persecutions of Nero and Diocletian. Their aim was the promotion of the Pure Gnostic Gospel or Pure Word of Jesus. The Scripture provided no justification for a Pope, they claimed. And, they maintained that they possessed the true secret of

1

Christianity, which had been passed to them by direct transmission from the Apostles through Jesus.

The Cathars called their church AMOR ('love') and claimed they possessed a spiritual technology originally taught by Jesus. Their 'heresy' (meaning 'choice', 'selection') concerned their use of this technology to transform themselves into higher beings.

Today, as I documented in my book *Cloak of the Illuminati*,[1] a convergence of technologies led by nanotechnology married to DNA is taking this 'heresy' to the next level and carrying us into a new age of Light. A major overhaul of the human body is not only conceivable; it is doable... and patentable. A thousand things that have doomed the fragile human body could change overnight.

Nanotechnology focuses on the creation of materials at nearly an atomic level -- nanocomputers are small enough that several hundred of them could fit inside the space of the period at the end of this sentence.

As I write these words on October 17, 2003 the Bush Administration requested $849 million of seed money to fund the United States' Nanotechnology Initiative. A report attached to the budget touts 'nano' as the next industrial revolution.

This is a mass understatement.

This initiative is an invisible reckoning, a tsunami wave of change that shrinks technology almost to the vanishing point. It will make science fiction reality.

According to the National Science Foundation, nanotechnology will be a $1 trillion industry by 2015. Every top government agency is involved in this revolution. However, the Pentagon ⬠ is the leading force in this endeavor.

Nanotechnology is essential to winning the War on Terror, says the Office of Science and Technology (a war the Pentagon believes will last decades). Ambitious plans are in the works.

Just before the US led rocking and lonely occupation of the cradle of civilization, came an announcement from *MIT News* of a revolutionary idea from the heads at the Pentagon and MIT's newly baptized Institute for Soldier Nanotechnologies (ISN). Launched with an initial grant of $50 million from the Pentagon and another $40 million from industry ISN will use nanotechnology to create the super soldier of the future.

The Pentagon and MIT plan to revolutionize the battle uniform worn by US forces by cloaking soldiers in a chameleon-like skin coated with smart nanotechnology materials that could help shield soldiers against bullets and chemical agents, and monitor their life support systems. Fibers could be used to carry fluids, emit signals, or change shape or color all in the same piece of clothing.

MIT's "coat of many colors" or miracle garment will have microbe-killing power and will even heal those who are wounded.

Another component – the number one request of soldiers, says MIT – is that it will be lightweight and waterproof. Soldiers want to be amphibious.

They plan on embedding "exo muscles" in this 'fish skin', giving the soldier Spider-Man-like strength. The soldiers would also wear exo-boots that would build up a charge of energy so that, if needed, a vertical leap of 20 feet would be possible.

An even more advanced suit made of a fabric as thin as a wet suit and strong as steel loaded with *self-reconfigurable* nanotechnology robots designed so that they can *change their external shape without human intervention* is possible with this technology.

Linked to the eyes in the sky and directly wired to the Net, this *e*-soldier I call the MIT *e*-Man (*e* = all 'wired' or computer-related technology) will be armed with the lethal power of newly developed electromagnetic weapons of focused mass destruction. (At the same time, reports the *Village Voice*, morning after pills are being developed to inhibit the effects of hardwired fear and 'softening' any possible remorse for the soldier's actions.)

The $170 million budget request for the Defense Advanced Research Projects Agency in fiscal 2005 includes $120 million for exploring and developing technological breakthroughs "that exist at the intersection of biology, information technology and micro/physical sciences" – that's cyborg or MIT *e*-Man technology -- according to the agency's budget request. This is only the beginning of the development of a fully programmable, remote-controlled super human warrior, a new 'Master Race'.

And one more thing, the MIT *e*-Man (*Mighty Man*) will be capable of manipulating light to render the soldier all but invisible. That's right, the super cloak will have fleshy 'scales' so that, like water, the uniform would blend into or scale to whatever background might be giving the soldier a cloaking capability. Like the aliens portrayed in the movies *Signs* and *Predator*, the MIT *e*-Man will be a cloaked killing machine.

This doped-up, *e* fire-spitting, bullet stopping, building jumpin' Jack Flash of a super soldier -- the 'MIT e Man' -- gives new meaning to the term "dressed to kill."

He (and she) will appear within the space of the next two decades, says MIT.

Not since Pallas-Athena, the Greek goddess of war and wisdom, donned her helmet of invisibility (also worn by Hermes), took up her Gorgon shield that turned men to stone and shook her spear of light has the world seen such a figure.

Until this new Super Soldier (or Super Zombie) is presented to us in a carefully storyboarded campaign like the President-as-a-flight-suit-clad cowboy making a Top Gun landing on the deck of an aircraft carrier proclaiming Independence Day and victory over the aliens most will not appreciate the enormity of this development in human evolution. However, once this Trojan horse leaves its first nano-footprint on the soil of our bright Blue Apple, as it leaps over tall buildings, things will never be the same.

The MIT *e*-Man project is part of an even larger government initiative. Coinciding with the announcement of the MIT *e*-Man came a draft government report saying we will alter human evolution, meaning the human body, within 20 years by combining what we know of the embryonic crafts of nanotechnology, biotechnology, information technology and cognitive sciences – the four primary 21st century Power Tools.[2] The building blocks of these Power Tools are bits, neurons, genes and atoms. With

5

these Power Tools we will create a new and improved human body, a new product of the human (r)evolution.

The 405-page report sponsored by the US National Science Foundation and Commerce Department, *Converging Technologies for Improving Human Performance*, calls for a broad-based research program to improve human performance leading to telepathy, machine-to-human communication, amplified personal sensory devices and enhanced intellectual capacity. It recommends ` heavily promoting the concept of the hive mind, the brave new *e* civilization.

RETURN TO BABYLON

 Soon after reading the announcements of the US government's pursuit of the MIT *e*-Man technology came reports of US soldiers entering the ancient gateway of Babylon. I kept thinking how the Pentagon's quest for the coat of many colors uncannily parallels the ancient quest for the Cloak or skin of the Mighty Man by the ancient Sumerian king, Nimrod.

NMRD, *Ni-Meru-Rod* or *Nimrod* when the vowels are added, was a second millennium B.C. Sumerian king who called himself "Mighty Man by the grace of Yahweh" and created an army of Mighty Men.

According to the Bible, Nimrod claimed royal descent from the Anunnaki gods of Iraq.[3,4,5] They are the Shining Ones, the mysterious angels of the pre-flood civilization described in Genesis 6 the Hebrews called Watchers, who gave birth to the Sons of the Gods or Goddesses, the warring *Nefilim* giants also described in Genesis 6, "they were the *Mighty Men* who are of Old, the People of the *Shem* (Renown, Highward)." Though they were around at the time of Adam, it appears that this race escaped the cataclysm that destroyed the first race of man who interbred with the Nefilim. Numerous researchers, led by Sitchin, claim these Mighty Ones possessed advanced technology, including military technology, which, says Sitchin, they employed in wars between gods and men.

Nimrod's title, "Mighty Man" was a title bestowed by Enlil (the Anunnaki Lord of the Command or Word) upon kings appointed by him. The means by which Nimrod became a "Mighty Man" is described in the *Book of Jasher* (the addendum to the Old Testament mentioned in the books of Joshua and Samuel but 'lost' or banned by the Church) and *The Book of the Generations of Man*, which says *the skins* that God made for Adam and his wife went to Enoch after their death, then to Methuselah, then to Noah (who survived the Flood), then Ham stole them and gave them to Cush (or Nimrod).[6] Sitchin asserts that the Anunnaki lord of technology E.A. or Enki manufactured the human body.[7] He also created the 'skin' transmitted to *Nimrod* who became *strong* when he put on the "magic" garments. Jasher 27:1-11 says that *Esau*, the brother of Jacob, kills Nimrod and takes Adam's skins (*c.* 1600 B.C).

This skin or garment of Adam was said to be a garment of light that came from the celestial realms.

The legends of the Jews assure us that putting on this cloak of light worked for Nimrod in a big way. He got tremendous results. It was by virtue of owning this garment that Nimrod was able to claim power to rule over the whole earth, and that he sat in his tower while men came and worshipped him. This tower, built in Babylon, was called the *Babel*, the Gate to God, and was the symbol of a human revolt or rebellion, which led to building a fortified tower that reached into the heavens in the course of staging revenge against the Hebrew god Yahweh (the Sumerian god Enlil), lest he flood the world again.

After Yahweh destroyed this tower and separated humanity by language,[8] the meaning of the word 'babel' was changed to 'nonsense', confusion'. The secrets of the gate and the cloak of the Mighty Man went underground.

While some may dismiss the correlation between the modern MIT *e*-Man and the skin of the Mighty Man of the past as merely literary contrivance or coincidence, such a view does not take into account the way in which the archetypal symbols, dramas and figures of history are recycled, if not repeating. We accept that this happens in symbol-rich Hollywood when a classic movie is remade, but it happens in the 'real' world of human consciousness too, according to a theory of archetypes introduced by Swiss psychiatrist and Gnostic champion Dr. C.G. Jung. It is important that we recognize the appearance of these archetypes for their ancient prototypes can provide sure guidance. The power of archetypal myth is enormous.

Whether they realize it or not the Pentagon, and those who control its activity, is on the leading edge of a profound development in human evolution that, if we're not careful, will make gods out of mere humans.

With this possibility in mind, in *Cloak of the Illuminati*, I ventured into the sea of memories, the mythological realm, and fished out additional examples of quests for ancient power skins or cloaks of the Illumined Ones.

One of the more interesting parallels the skin of the MIT *e*-Man draws with ancient power cloaks concerns the Cloak or *Pallium* conferred upon Elisha by Elijah just before his departure to the heavens in a "whirlwind", *c.* 800 B.C.[9]

The 12th century Winchester Psalter illustrates the baptism of Jesus by John the Baptist, while an angel waits, holding a cloak symbolizing Jesus' 'new life' through baptism.

The key to the Pallium is to know that it transferred or transmitted Elijah's *prophetic* or *oracular* power to Elisha, who was appointed to replace Elijah as the leader of the prophets or oracles, and to complete the spiritual mission of

Elijah.[10] The illumination from the 12th century Winchester Bible on the previous page illustrates the belief that this cloak or Robe of Glory was transmitted to Jesus. *Webster's* says *illuminati* is a term for a newly baptized Christian initiate.[11] When Jesus dons the cloak of light provided by John he becomes an Illumined One. According to Christian tradition, Elijah later appeared as John the Baptist and, Christians believe, he will return as the herald of the Second Coming. Perhaps he'll seek his cloak.

The whirlwind is a key story element linking Elijah's Pallium to the goddess Mari's *Pala* garment. The word *Pala*, notes Sitchin, is the name given to the cloak of the illumined goddess Mari in Syria.[12] *Pala* means 'miracle', 'wonderful', 'shining', 'magnificent', 'hidden'[13] and 'to vibrate' and 'to hurl', according to 19th century symbolist Major-General J.G.R. Forlong.[14] Mari wore the Pala garment along with her *Shugurra* helmet that Sitchin says 'took her far into the universe'.[15]

The International Standard Bible Encyclopedia connects the etymology of *nepîlîm* with this garment, claiming Nephilim comes from *niphal* and the verb *pala*, meaning "be extraordinary," i.e., "extraordinary being."

This mysterious Cloak of Light is the magnificent miracle garment worn in modified form by the most extraordinary beings, the spiritual giants of their day, including Osiris, Enki, Mari, Nimrod, Enoch, Joseph (of the Coat of Many Colors), Aaron, Elijah, John the Baptist, Jesus, and others. Each of these figures displayed gigantic feats, many of which were associated with their clothing. They also were considered masters of the four divine forces

10

or elements of *earth, air, fire* and *water*. The general term for these figures was *Oracle*.

According to E.A. Wallis Budge, a few of the many powers possessed by the cloak-clad Oracle include healing the sick, cloaking his companions in an "incorruptible" body, manipulation of matter, and predicting the future.[16]

John Rossner, Ph. D. has claimed the Oracle practiced a "divine alchemy," the goal of which was self-transformation and the transformation of humanity towards a divine state of being and to "become for a time as mighty as the original possessor of the power."[17] The "apotheosized" or "divinized" human heroes, the Oracles, were described as "new beings". They are the gods and goddesses of the four divine elements of earth, air, fire and water.

It is synchronistic the way the four elements of the ancient world match up with the four Power Tools of 21st century science – genes, bits, neurons and atoms. It's as if the archetypal four divine forces of the ancients are being re-tooled or re-vealed in our New Age of Light.

Archetypically speaking, these four Power Tools coincide with the *four* 'books' of magic assigned to the 'Oracle of Oracles', Thoth or Hermes (who also wore the cloak). We are told in the magical texts that *'These are the titles of the four books:*

1. *The old book;*
2. *The book to destroy men;*
3. *The great book;*
4. *The book to be as a God'.*[18]

11

The four elemental types, symbolized by the Lion, Bull, Man and Eagle were given as symbols of the one God. In all lands, in all languages are found endless myths of the Sacred Four. These elements change over time depending upon the conceptions of the civilization. Always, they are best manipulated by the Oracle, who carries a message of love and reverence, and combines the elements to lead us into the Great Beyond ('Hyperborea').

In ancient Egypt the rod of Ptah was the emblem of the four divine forces. It is called the TET, after the god Thoth, That or TET, the Moon god, who was the great Craftsman who made the Ark of Ptah or the Ship of the Gods. A four-tiered tower symbolized the TET. In the language of symbolism the four-tiered TET is equivalent to the four-armed or strutted cross ✝ or Tree of Life upon which Jesus was crucified.

As we will explore in detail later, in the ancient sacred sciences the Oracle was the master of a fifth force; the *Quintessence*, or the biblical Word that mediated the four divine forces. Plato symbolized this fifth force by the dodecahedron . In October 2003, *Nature* magazine published an article claiming the universe is shaped like a dodecahedron. God 'painted' with it at the time of creation, said Plato. The dodecahedron, I propose, is the logo of the God Head and the Oracle. It encodes the science of transmutation.

The secret teachings of the Gnostic mystery schools of all the ages have professed the same truth. In our inner core, in our spiritual essence we are soul-star stuff. We are divine, noble or true blue particle-rays of light, *quantum* ships asail in the Cosmic Ocean of Resonance, cast a drift like crystal flakes of snow in a (*dodecahedral-shaped*

) snow globe after experiencing the Great Shake until appeared the globe of Earth sailing about in the Milky Way.

Traveling as emissaries from the Source of creation our souls become bottled-up, clothed, or cloaked in a body or container intricately woven from coils of DNA that is essentially a complex and dense living energy pattern composed of the four 'elements': *earth, air, fire* and *water*. The soul enters a sleeping state in the body, as if it is walking around in a dream, just as in the children's rhyme.

> '*Row, row, row the boat,*
> *Gently down the stream.*
> *Merrily, merrily, merrily, merrily,*
> *Life is but a dream.*'

The object of earth life, according to the Gnostic texts we will examine, is to achieve Gnosis, to wake up, discover the secrets of the fifth divine force, put on the Cloak and fill the shoes of the Oracle. Today, the four 21st-century Power Tools will offer significant advantages and will have a profound impact on the spiritual life of Gnosis seekers. As Shimon Peres, former prime minister of Israel,

13

observed, "That which has been achieved by the atomic bomb in the field of military strategy will be accomplished in the future by nanotechnology in the field of civil potential." It will happen quickly.

Toward this end, Australian nanotechnologist Josh Hall imagines a "magic living cloud" he calls "Utility Fog" composed of nano robots in the shape of *dodecahedrons*

[19] These 'assemblers' are capable, voila, of programmable construction of any desired atomically perfect product, given feedstock, energy, and instructions. It has a body about the size of a human cell and 12 arms sticking out in all directions. A bucketful of such robots might form a "robot crystal" by linking their arms up into a lattice structure.

Now take a room, with people, furniture, and other objects in it - it's still mostly empty air. Fill the air completely full of robots and it will fill the space with whatever one's heart desires.

Christianity has angels and the Holy Spirit that act in mysterious ways. Gnostic Christians assert that it was a lower order of angels who built their heaven upon the confines of matter, and that they molded it into a habitable world, and then created a race of beings to inhabit it. Nanotechnologists visualize billions of assemblers doing the same job. Critics say talk of such assemblers is hype and will not happen in the foreseeable future. In my opinion, these critics are taking the last gasps of breath from a rapidly disappearing world of controllable science.

14

Here's a short list of the powers one would have if living in the living nano fog.

Creation: the ability to manifest or unmanifest objects on command.

Levitation: the ability to cause objects to move in the air.

Manipulation: the ability to move objects at a distance.

Teleportation: the ability to beam from place to place.

Alchemy: the ability to transmute any element into another, for instance water into wood.

Like the NSF report on the future 'MIT e-human', Josh Hall's nano-fog provides the makings of a figure whose enhanced attributes were acknowledged by the ancients and ascribed to the Oracles, highly evolved spiritual beings who wore the Pala or Miracle Cloak of the Mighty Ones and who knew the secrets of the four cosmic forces of creation, plus the fifth, could invoke these forces, duplicate their effects and predict the outcome. In addition, the Oracle could connect with the Source.

It didn't take long for eyeglasses to catch on. It likely will be the same with this new skin or Cloak of Light. The platform for the re-introduction of this being is the creation of a new human skin loaded with technology that transforms an ordinary human into a being of extraordinary military potential. Will this technology also be used to create a skin of light of the Oracle that transforms an ordinary human into a being of enhanced and magnificent spiritual potential as well? What will our world be like when millions of people wear this advanced technology and display superhuman capabilities?

We'll begin with an over view of Gnostic teaching and an assessment of the Gnostic view of the Oracle. The goal of the Gnostic belief system is to obtain the light, illumination, self realization -- realization of self as soul, stripped of the body, emotions, and mind -- not an intellectual awareness, but the actual *experience* of self realization.

The second goal is God realization, connection with the God Head. This encompasses *All* knowledge and is far beyond anything the mind can grasp and is impossible to describe. It can only be experienced.

As we shall see, when the Gnostics put on the cloak of light they let go of their earthly attachments and attained Gnosis by activating an inner divine spark or *scintilla* called the Blue Stone, the Blue Light, the Blue Tone, the Blue Pearl or the Blue Apple.

Our English word pearl is derived from Sanskrit, meaning "pure." The Blue Apple, as it is called in the Languedoc region of southern France, home of the Cathars ('the *Pure*'), is seen in the inner eye. With a lot of practice it can be followed into higher states of consciousness. Gnosis states that many can travel (out of body) into the higher realms, but to reach the pure land of AMOR, the pure spiritual worlds beyond time, space, matter and energy (the four nuclear forces) one must go through such a deep zone of darkness that it is impossible to traverse unless one is guided by the Blue Light. It takes a Living Master, an Oracle, to link the student with the blue light and the inner sounds that lead the student to the higher states of awareness. One wonders how this Oracle will manifest in our New Age of Light.

16

2.
THE RETURN OF SOPHIA

In December 1945, two peasants, Muhammed and Khalifah Ali were digging for fertilizer at the base of the Jabal al-Tarif cliff about 7 miles north-east of Nag Hammadi, Egypt, in the Nile River Valley.[1] They tethered their camels to a boulder, and came upon a buried red jar as they were digging around the base of the boulder. Muhammed Ali told scholar J.M.Robinson that at first he was afraid to break the jar -- the lid may have been sealed with bitumen, as a blackish substance is present on the lid -- for fear a jinn ('spirit') might be inside, but the thought that gold might be contained instead, he broke it with his mattock. Out flew particles of papyrus.

Inside the sealed jar, which lay undisturbed for seventeen centuries, was a collection of thirteen codices containing over fifty texts, including a few Hermetic discourses and a copy of Plato's *Republic*, originally written in Greek, and later translated into Coptic (Egyptian Christian). The collection of books also included among them *The Gospel of Thomas* and the *Gospel of Truth*, and belonged to the earliest "mainstream" Christians.

Ali wrapped his books in his tunic and took them home, to his hovel in the hamlet of al-Qasr. The books, loose covers and loose pages were dumped in the straw, next to the oven. Thinking the books were worthless, or maybe

17

even unlucky to have, Ali's widowed mother burned part of the books. Muhammed deposited the books with a local Coptic priest, Basiliyus Abd al-Masih. The priest's wife had a brother, Raghib Andrawus, who went from village to village teaching English and history in the local Coptic (Egyptian Christian) church schools. He came to visit, and, on seeing one of the books, recognized it might be valuable and took it to Cairo. There he showed it to a Coptic physician interested in the Coptic language, George Sobhi, who called in the authorities from the Department of Antiquities. They seized the book, agreeing to pay Raghib a sum for the books. The book was deposited in the museum, according to the register, on October 4, 1946.

Today all the Nag Hammadi codices are in the Coptic Museum in Cairo. (The first codex of the Nag Hammadi library found in 1945 was purchased and given to Dr. Carl G. Jung on his eightieth birthday in 1952. It is called the Codex Jung. It was later returned to Egypt, where it is kept in the Coptic Museum, Cairo, with the other volumes.)

The full collection was finally published, after ugly scholarly turf wars, under the auspices of the Department of Antiquities of the Arab Republic of Egypt in Conjunction with the United Nations Educational, Scientific and Cultural Organization by Brill between 1972 and 1984 as the *Facsimile Edition of the Nag Hammadi Codices*. The Christian world was stunned to learn that the 'real' or 'pure' Jesus presented in this library does not match the invented Jesus of modern Christian tradition.

The Nag Hammadi texts represent *the central secrets of Jesus's Gnosticism*, the Gnostic "Way not taken" by the assemblers and compilers of the Christian canon ("rule") at the Council of Nicea in 325 AD (which spawned the Nicean Creed and the concept of original sin).

The goal of the secret teachings of Jesus was to rewire and liberate our consciousness so that we could see past the illusions of Earth life and connect with the God Head, the means by which is already hidden within us. According to Gnostic teaching, the purpose of mortal existence is to reclaim the skin of light, re-enter the gate of Eden and dwell in the Garden of Life. All else is death. Find that gate and we shall live forever in bliss. Concerning the Garden, the Gnostics taught that in the Garden stands the holy *Tree of Life*. High in its branches sings a *bird*. Listen for the voice of the bird, for when you are properly aligned with Heaven and Earth, she will tell you all things.

This bird (usually a dove) is a symbol for Sophia, the Holy Spirit, or the Wisdom. When this Wisdom comes, she will lead one into all Truth.

The reason why modern Christians may not have heard of this Way is because, like the Cathars who attempted to revive the pure teachings of Jesus in the 13th century, its teachers were brutally murdered or driven into exile. Its books were condemned, destroyed or vanished from sight. Simply, appallingly, as a result of a cover-up of the actual teachings of Jesus begun more than seventeen hundred years ago the real Jesus is considered the greatest heretic to modern Christians. We must also recognize that today's dictionaries and accepted translations of Greek words, and even thesauruses, also reflect the impostor Judaeo-Christian worldview, which is a product of that same council. As history shows, if the meanings of words (such as the word Christ) are changed a people can be conquered, enslaved.

In order to more fully appreciate the Nag Hammadi texts a brief sketch of the historical backdrop in which they were buried is necessary. The first two centuries AD in Egypt was a time of revolt and insurrection against the corrupt Roman rule. The Romans ruthlessly persecuted the participants in the Jesus revolution (as did other so-called Christians).

Within a hundred years of the death of Jesus Christianity had already separated into two broad divisions, represented on the one side by the followers of Peter, the orthodox Jew, and on the other side by the followers of Paul, the Gnostic "heretic" who was struck by a beam of light. In the second century the division grew even larger. The *Christian* Gnostics came into existence and now the division was between the Orthodox *Church* and the *Gnostic Heresy*. On one side stood knowledge on the other stood faith. In these power struggles Jesus was lost.

The Christian Gnostics were the offshoots and products of the three great Gnostic Schools of that day, Schools which had been in existence for centuries, and which formed the basis of the original Christian synthesis of religious experience. The essential teaching of these Schools was this: because human beings are conscious beings, it was believed by Jesus and the Gnostic Christians that our destiny is to develop our superhuman spiritual abilities and to make contact with divine consciousness. In essence, our destiny is to make contact with the God Head

(called the Pleroma)   or God Consciousness. A massive effort was underway to harmonize, synthesize or *syncreticize* (cross-link) the wisdom teachings and mythologies of the ancients and to formulate a procedure to put on the Cloak of Light (Mari's Pala garment), a symbol of unfolding divinity and metamorphosis into a divine being.

The first of these Schools, located in Alexandria, Egypt, the shining pearl of the Mediterranean, was one of those in which Jesus himself had studied during his residence in Egypt.[2] Mark was supposed to have brought the Gospel to Alexandria from AD 45 to 62. Just south of the city of Alexandria, perched high upon a lofty plateau overlooking the blue waters of Lake Mareotis, there had lived for centuries before the Christian era, a group of men and women devoted to esoteric study and meditation. They are considered both a branch of the Pythagorean Essenes and teachers of the influential Hindu-Buddhist Theravada school, then living in the Bible lands, and were known as the *Therapeutae* ("to heal") or *Jessians*. They are the first group of Christian Gnostics. For Philo the therapeutae were the theoreticians and the Essenes the practitioners. Philo writes that the Essenes in Palestine and Syria were identical with the *Magi* in Persia and the *gymnosophists* (the wise men) in India. They are Oracles who could patch into the Consciousness of God (called the *matrix* today). New studies say that the Essenes, also called *Kanobi*, relied heavily on a cannabis extract to baptize and to heal.[3]

The second great Gnostic School of the second century was located in the city of Ephesus in Syria. It concerned itself mainly with the comparative study of religion and philosophy. In this School the philosophies of ancient Sumeria, India, Babylon and Persia were commingled with those of Plato and Pythagoras, and the teachings of the Buddha were compared with those of the Jewish Kabalists (and likely the Tarot, 'the royal Way or Path' that leads the Fool or initiate on his path to enlightenment and through the Gate to God). In the preceding century Apollonius of Tyana, a prophet and miracle worker often compared with Jesus, had established his own esoteric School in this city, adding its strength to the exoteric work of the College.

The great College of Ephesus was a focus of the universal secret doctrines. Apollonius was not the only charismatic miracle worker. He is considered one of several 'divine men' -- people who were considered to be patched into the God Head, and who sought to reform the religious practices of their age. They were called "oracle mongers" by the jealous established religious authorities.[4]

Central to the religious belief of Greeks and Romans at the end of the second century, the reign of the Roman Philosopher Emperor Marcus Aurelius, was the idea that there was a special group of 'divine men' between the eternal gods and the ordinary mortals, people who combined philosophy and sacred science to cure ill persons, and who transmitted knowledge of how to become divine. One of the central tenets of this philosophical school was that there were three types of beings, mortals, gods and 'beings in between', who like Pythagoras, were called 'philosophers' ('*lovers of Sophia*') or what I will refer to as the Oracle.

The concept of the miracle-working Oracle played an important role in the rise of Christianity. The first Christians were Jews who believed in the imminent appearance of a Messiah who was a mortal teacher and/or a military leader who could explain the Law of Moses correctly and restore Israel to pre-eminence. Many of these converts believed that Jesus had been some kind of 'divine man' or Oracle whose divine attributes transcended the Jewish messiah.

It was from this School that spread much of the Gnostic teaching which drove the rulers of the orthodox Church to great acts of ugliness and evil in order to squelch it. The men who came out of this School were equipped with *knowledge of the Oracle,* and therefore were considered as deadly enemies by those who were attempting to cloak the consciousness of humanity with a politico-religious structure dependent on faith and led by political and military (false or 'fascist') messiahs. Such a Church, founded on power, had no use, except as war games fodder, for those who took personal responsibility for their spiritual advancement and who sought the true secrets of the Burning Bush (which center around some mysterious blue stones of enlightenment).

In contrast to the Church formed in his name, Jesus had valued the acceptance of self-knowledge (second to the doctrine of Unconditional Love) as a means to promote responsibility for one's own life, actions and thinking. Like the Buddha ('the Awakened One'), Jesus opposed the priests, politicians and theologians who barred the way to true self-knowledge, to maintain their influence. In the *Gospel of Thomas* Jesus flatly says: "The Pharisees and the Scribes took the keys of knowledge and they hid them. Neither did they enter, nor did they allow those who wished to enter. But you become *wise as serpents, and innocent as doves.*"[5]

Wise as serpents, you say? The third Gnostic group, also situated in Alexandria, which exerted a powerful influence upon budding Gnostic Christianity, was the sect known as the *Ophites*, or the People of the Serpent. We will look into this group in detail. *Ophion* was a divine serpent who lived in the Tree of Life in the primordial Garden, and who revealed the sacred Mysteries against the will of the jealous god. His symbol was the serpent's egg or stone of many bright colors.[6] The etymology of the word shows *Ops* is power and dominion; *Opulens* is wealthy; *Opus* is work; *(s)Ophia* is wisdom; *Optics* "I see" is the serpent power; *Optimum* is the best; *Open* is the door.

Their emblems reveal that Cathars adopted the Ophite serpent symbolism. The meaning of the symbol spit from the serpent ☓ (shown in the Cathar crosses on the next page) was threefold: it represented, first, Supreme *Wisdom* (Gnosis); second, those Perfected Men who are the embodiments of *Power* (the Oracle); third, the Christos-principle (or Particle) within each man himself: the divine Ego made One with Gnosis (*Light*). Wisdom. Power. Light. These are the goals of the Gnostic quest.

The horn with three rays at the base of the cross is the symbol for the Three Light Rays that are found in Egyptian hieroglyphs. This horn, fabled to be hidden underneath the sacred Tree of Paradise, is the symbol for the music that calls the Spirit of Sophia.[7]

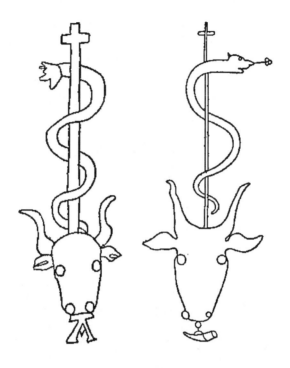

Cathar crosses. The bull's head is the symbol for Osiris, the Ark of the Covenant and the letter M, all of which we

will discuss as we continue. The horn *with the three rays symbolizes Power, Wisdom and Light.*

In Greece, the goddess *Pallas*-Athena or Pallas-ATONA (600 B.C.) was patroness of the serpent born and a likely inspiration to the Ophites. Her spear of light, made by the god Hephaestus (the Sumerian Enki), lord of smith craft (technology, alchemy), was the same as the Tree of Light in the Garden. It enabled her to 'lift the serpent', ala Moses and the Cathar cross, and to heal and protect her people. Probably through Enki's alchemy she became an Oracle, who lifted the secrets of light, symbolized in art by a wavy line 〰️ , 〰️ (and a particle or dot • when viewed face-on), and placed her people in *accord* (a chord) with nature.

Athena emerging from the 'head' of Zeus while Hephaestus/Enki assists.

The golden Pallas-Athena. From the Parthenon, Nashville, TN. Coiled at the base of her spear is the serpent out of which the Greeks, who called themselves the serpent born, emerged.

27

According to Greek myth, Athena was born from the 'head' of Zeus. Obviously, this is an important metaphor. When we pull on the thread of this 'oracular' symbolism, we find that, generally speaking, the 'head' symbolizes *Divine Force*.[8] Intriguingly, the Divine Force is symbolized

by the three rays or rings of light ♀ spit from the serpent of wisdom ∿ , ∿ , • in Cathar symbolism (and posing at the feet of Athena on the previous page).

The spherical shape of the human head ○ , according to Plato, likens it to the universe, the circle or *ring* or *song* of life. In Greek tradition, concentric rings ◎ stand for the meeting place between the terrestrial world and the other world.[9] This is the definition of an *oracular center*, the dot of real estate where the Oracle climbs the *tower* or Tree of Life and brings the Divine Force – called the Holy Apples in the *Zohar* -- down to Earth. Following the path of this symbolism, we find that when the Divine Force (Gnosis),

• , is added to the head ○ , we form the sacred   *eye* or

circle symbol ⊙ , meaning *sun* and *gold* in Egyptian hieroglyphics. Gold, of course, is the object of the alchemist's quest. In alchemical symbolism *gold* (*Sol*, sun) and *soul* are interchangeable, meaning the purification of the soul, the polishing of the inner pearl, was the real subject and object of the alchemist's *Opus*.

28

Like rubbing the edge of a crystal bell, the alchemist begins working on their consciousness and a vibration begins to sing in their bodies. The inner eye opens. A lost spiritual Cloak of Light manifests and encircles ⊙ the body with a new 'skin' composed of a ring or tone. The perfect pitch, the perfect resonance, we know, and the Divine Particle alights; the soul will sail home effortlessly, like Ellie in *Contact* sailing through the galaxy in a serpent rope or wormhole or, *flash* (!), dematerializing and teleporting like the *USS Eldridge* back to home port.

It is not easy to achieve.

The entire underlying theory of alchemy is that *something* must be developed within and *secreted* from the human body, which will enable the seeker to make oneself over into a golden one, a Shining One, an Oracle.

As the French alchemist Fulcanelli said:

'The secret of alchemy is that there exists a means of manipulating matter and energy so as to create what modern science calls a *force field*. This force field acts upon the observer and puts him in a privileged position in relation to the universe. From this privileged position he has access to realities that space and time, matter and energy, normally conceal from us. This is what we call the Great Work.'[10]

The Oracle possesses the secret of the Great Opus, the secret of secreting this Divine Force field that turns base metal into gold, that brings new light into the world and regenerates it to its original condition as a paradise.

Pushing the circumference of this Gnosis ● we find that, today, ◉ , an eye with a dilated pupil, is used on maps to indicate different types of *centers from which energy and/or communication emanate: central station, lighthouse, transformer station, post office, telegraph and telephone station* and *pushbutton* (for on/off).[11]

Tabulating the varied symbolic meanings of the 'head' in the goddess of wisdom Athena's story suggests that she was 'born' from (or upon) a tone or light of creation at an oracular power center ◉ . The Gnostics said Sophia (wisdom) was born on a ray of light.

In fact, Athena's oracle, the Akropolis ('place of secrets') or Arkropolis (place of the Ark/Arch) in Athens, Greece and duplicated in Nashville, Tennessee, is called *Petra Makra*, "the Abyss," or cave. Literally translated, *Petra Makra* is "Maker's Stone".[12] This Stone is, in essence, a regenenerative tone or vibration, a force field.

Nearly all ancient religions worshipped a stone of light or *pe-tra* (Pa-Tara means 'stone of enlightenment'), a serpent stone of the Oracle, which fell from heaven that is guarded by a serpent (or cloaked by a force field or a tone ∿ , ∿ , ●?). Acquisition of this (s)tone brings superhuman abilities and connection to all of creation.

This tradition can be traced to the Sumerian story of the ME tablets of civilization delivered by the wise serpent god Enki, and later 'lifted' or stolen by Mari. Also known as Is-

Tara ('compassion', 'enlightenment'), Mari was an illumined goddess who operated the *Palla-dium* pillar called the *Ash-Tara* (*Is-Tara* or *Ashera*) in 1 Kings 13. Her interaction with it, as portrayed here in this Assyrian seal (1049-609 B.C.), illuminates the meaning of Athena, Moses and all other Oracles lifting the serpent of miracle light and bringing a Divine Force Field of possibility, protection and prosperity to their people.

Is-Tara or Mari at her pillar. This pillar of the Oracle, the **i**, *is the* ⊙ *when viewed from the top down.*

By following the symbolism of the flying serpent, this pillar, we will see, increased the amount of a 'miracle' substance called celestial Life Force (*manna, ether* or *subtle matter*), originally ejected from the Milky Way's 'G-Spot' or 'G-Zone', at a given place on Earth, enhancing the spiritual capabilities of the people. Oracles throughout the ages have been describing this Pillar as a way to stimulate and awaken the 'G-Spot' and the secret energy of the Goddess, hidden as it is like butter hidden in milk, in various luminous ways.

The *Zohar* says that the serpent that seduced Eve was a kind of *Flying Camel*.[13] This is exactly what we see in the Assyrian depiction of Is-Tara. An *M*-shaped serpent that has *two-humps*, like a camel, and two 'heads' enters or exits a pillar. This shape is duplicated in a Cathar symbol as , meaning 'yoke of Christ'.[14] Arabians called the two-humped camel the "ship of the desert." Curiously, there appears to be some form of a winged ship floating above Is-Tara's pillar. Further exploring the magnificent mystery of the flying M or camel shape of the serpent takes us to the heart of the secrets of the Gnostic Oracle.

THE MYSTERIOUS M

By far the most sacred of all letters to the Kabbalists was M, which Bayley says was regarded as both masculine and feminine.[15] In addition to the yoke symbol the Cathars show the serpent with the head symbol ◯ attached to the

shape of a letter M as such, 𝓂, forming another shape strikingly similar in shape to the flying serpent or 'M' in the Tara depiction.

The M may have been viewed as both masculine and feminine, and portrayed with two heads, because it is the fusion of twin serpents or lines (the Cathar designers identified the Twin Circles ⅄ with X, the Latin numeral for *Ten*, *A ten* or *A Tone*). Twin spirals that 'oppose' one another, but are actually One, ◡, ◯ also represent this concept of the combined masculine and feminine. Rubbed together, these two sticks create 'fire'.

Two spirals or two lines forming an X signify oneness.

In Gnostic terms the twin spirals or serpents are called *Aeons*. The coupling or union of Aeons is the *source of creation*, a concept reflected in the Egyptian paired *neters* (god-principles) and in Tantric and Buddhist philosophy.

33

For thousands of years the *clockwise spiral* ideogram has been strongly associated with   *water, power* and outgoing *energy*.[16] Starting from the middle it forms a '*G*' (the Mayan term for 'love'). Its mirror (twin) image, or inversion, the spiral in its *counterclockwise rotation* , also a '*G*', appeared at approximately the same time.[17] It is an Egyptian hieroglyph for *thread*. A similar Chinese ideogram means *return* or *homecoming*.[18] The Tibetans painted the thread on the walls of their homes and gave it the meaning *home*,[19] the place one returns to.

According to Mayan metaphysicist Hunbatz Men, the letter '*G*' at the heart of each of the spirals stands for *egg, zero, essence* and *the Milky Way Galaxy* in Mayan symbolism.[20] The central Healing Sun of our galaxy is a sort of Cosmic '*G*' Spot that, properly stimulated, ejects a life regenerating substance in ongoing waves.

Every culture has a myth dealing with the creation of our galaxy. Since the Paleolithic times the beginning of life and the spreading of the vibrations from the Milky Way's Galactic Core has been described as the hatching of a Cosmic Egg laid by a *Great Mother Bird*. A germ shown as a dot • resided in the midst of this egg.[21] The beginning of life within the Cosmic Egg, it was believed, is caused by the orbiting of twin snakes   that are in cooperative opposition or atone-ment with one another.

The Cosmic (Serpent's) Egg is a female symbol for the universal womb or matrix of space-time. When this egg cracked open all life appeared. Brilliant cosmic energy or essence, the seed from which all life, including human, sprang into existence and fanned out in waves. The Egg is enveloped by *water*, symbolized in Paleolithic art by wavy lines 〰〰 or serpents.[22]

In the Mayan Milky Way symbolism, shown here, we see three G spirals. The G spawns a ladder or flight of stairs. Interspersed with the Mayan Gs are matching Cathar serpent Gs, standing for *Gnosis* and the *divine light*.

The Mayan G forms a ladder or stairway (left). Cathar G with the Scala Dei or Ladder to Heaven attached (right).

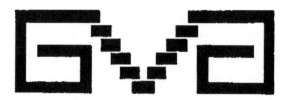

Two Gs 'spitting' 'ladders' facing each other form an M.

When facing each other the Gs form the letter M in this Mayan glyph. In my view, it represents the *union* of male and female, Heaven and Earth. The purpose of the flying camel is revealed. It is a conduit. The Cathar M will be examined momentarily and will reveal the same meaning.

As we can see, the Mayan and the Cathar serpent G symbols convey the same message: 'we know about the Milky Way and its G-Spot'. I would hypothesize that the Cathars and the Mayans drew from the same wisdom well as the Hindus who used the (orgasmic) expression OM, or

O ∕\/\/ , *O-mmmm*, to represent the vibrating or 'living' water or wisdom of life oozing from the Milky Way.

M, whether written *A U M* or OM, O ∕\/\/ or even ∕∖∕ , stands for 'light' and the *Um-bilicus*, the center or hub of life, the Source of all things, the *om-phalos* or place of the Oracle. By pre-Christian reckoning the Oracle was the temple of Mari-Is-Tara. Here, the goddess was shown with her mate -- a serpent, tree or cross -- ala the illustration on page 31.[23] She is the goddess connecting

36

Heaven and Earth through the M-shaped tube and bringing the pulse or hum of life to Earth. She is the Oracle.

What this fluid is, exactly, is Mother Nature's secret.

When captured or jarred up $\bigcirc$ /\/\/ becomes ⟨⟩. This expulsion is, I suspect, the Tone of God referred to as an *oil* and called *Chrestos* by the Essenes that Mari Magdalene kept in a 'jar'. In Egypt this seed sound was

Amon or *Amen*,[24] one of whose hieroglyphs ⟨⟩ was a serpent in an oval, mirroring the filaments (fil-*amen*-ts) in the jars from Hathor's temple at Denderah (Tan-Tara, Tantra), Egypt. It meant a pregnant belly.[25]

Mari was a 'god-maker' and a 'gold maker' who prepared humans on a mental, spiritual, physical and emotional level for the highest sensual experience: entering the conduit, the stargate, returning the soul to its Source. Interestingly, the elemental symbol for *gold* is Au. The alchemists hint that to make gold requires gold. Add the M or serpent power to A U, gold, and we have A U M, the tone of God. The alchemical process is revealed.

In many mythological systems the serpent, /\/\/ , is the symbol for "the hidden god" (*occult* in Latin). This is a pun. On one level the god is hidden in the sense that it is invisible. On another level, it is called hidden because its secrets are withheld from the people. Based upon the accumulation of our findings, we may hypothesize that this was the Divine Force, the hidden essence or miracle substance churned from the Milky Way by the Oracle that filled the human with an overpowering, overwhelming inclusive feeling that filled the body, the heart and the soul. Orthodox patriarchal priesthoods have always sought to exclude humanity from secrets of the Divine Force and the cosmic G-Spot. The Gnostics have always sought to reveal it. To touch it is fire.

I have gone into such painstaking detail about the M because the Cathars, who claimed Jesus taught them this symbol system, used this symbol -- ⌣⋀⋃⌣ -- the M or 'flying camel' -- to symbolize the "yoke" (or wisdom, Gnosis) of Christ. This 'yoke' connected them to Christ (a fact known by Leonardo da Vinci who painted an M between Jesus and Mary Magdalene in *The Last Supper*).

From this we deduce that once the Maker's Stone or Tone is in our head this vibration or key of life ties or yokes ⌣⋀⋃⌣ one to Heaven (*anna*). When it *hums* in the head (as it does in that of the Oracle) it connects one with *home* and liberates us from Earth.

In this Cathar symbol -- ⚭ -- the wisdom ⋀⋀ is in a head symbol with two eyes. It is combined with the cross, the symbol of ascent or the ladder to God that sticks out from the head like an antenna. I believe this symbol represents the presence of the tone of God in the head of the Cathar, who now is in direct contact with the God Head.

This symbolism is carried forward into the story of

John the Baptist, the Gnostic initiator of Jesus, i.e. the one who tied Jesus to the Light, who was known for wearing a *camel* ⌣ᒐ∿ᒐ⌣ hair raiment (*a-ray-ment*), cloak or coat (that he transmitted to Jesus). If we supposed that this camel hair is a pun for his body being cloaked or covered in the living wisdom waters or tones of the Great Deep (◯ ∿) it brings an interesting perspective to the claim that Jesus is God in the flesh (or is it *flash?*). Like John, he would be a human being cloaked in Godly substance (an *oily* substance called an *essence* or *effulgence*) and capable of sharing (transmitting or broadcasting) this substance, the Maker's tone, ∿ , with others. This means he is a *co-creator* with God.

I have traced the background of the M symbolism to the Zarathustran belief system introduced by the Iranian Oracle Zoroaster (628-551 B.C., the time of Buddha), who some believe is Nimrod, who, we recall, wore the skin of the Mighty Man. Zarathustra means "yellow camel" (zara = yellow, ushtra = camel)![26]

The later Zoroastrians, perhaps embarrassed by their prophet's primitive-sounding name, said that the name meant "*Golden Light,*" deriving their meaning from the word *zara* and the word *ushas*, light or dawn.

Others says the name Zoroaster comes from TzURA = a figure, and TzIUR = to fashion, ASh = fire, and STR = hidden; from these we get the words Zairaster = fashioning images of hidden fire; -- or Tzuraster = the image of secret things.[27] These meanings align the name Zoro-Aster or

39

Zoro-As-Tara with the Ash-Tara pillar of light, as well as

O ∕∿∕ and the Egyptian hidden god, Amen ⬭.

Like Akhenaton in 18th Dynasty Egypt, and Moses in *c.* 1400 B.C., Zarathrustra introduced the concept of monotheism -- the One Ring O ∕∿∕ --- in his time line.

Zoroaster called the One God *Ahura Mazda.* Zoroastrian lore was known in ancient Iran as the doctrine of the Magi, and it was they who came from the East to seek out the baby Jesus. The first mention of them in the Old Testament is in Jeremiah, 630 B.C., when they were in Nebuchadnezzar's retinue. The Chief Magi entered Jerusalem with him when he looted and leveled the Temple of Solomon in search of the power tools of the Temple.[28]

Ahura Mazda.

It is vital to note for our later discussion that *Ahura Mazda* (the "Wise Lord" and father of gods) has created six *Amesha Spentas* - divine entities - also called the *Beneficent (or Holy) Immortal Ones*. Following the death of Zarathustra/Zoroaster these six 'divine entities' were associated with six branches of creation: Fire; Ox; Metals; Earth; Water; and Plants. These divine entities also appear as *archangels* and *angels* in the Old Testament and in the Koran, which took over numerous aspects of the Old Testament. The seventh divine entity Ahura Mazda created is the *sacred spirit, Spenta Mainyu*. He is a divine entity, the greatest of all powers, the '*Sublime Constructive Force*', ◯ ∧∨. As is summarized by the priests in every Zoroastrian mass, *Spenta Mainyu* represents the '*God incarnate in man*' (therefore *Spenta Mainyu* may be rendered as *Serpent A-Men* ⌒ in Egyptian symbolism). Through *Spenta Mainyu's* association man becomes a *co-creator* with Ahura Mazda.

There are passages in the Essene documents found in the Dead Sea Scrolls, which seem to be directly borrowed from Zoroastrian sources. These texts describe the spirit of truth in conflict with the spirit of error, and a battle of the sons of light against the sons of darkness. This scenario later became part of Gnostic Christian mythology.

Continuing our survey of the background of Gnostic Christianity, in the next chapter we find that, in addition to the Greeks, Buddhists and Zoroastrians, the Gnostic Christians drew heavily from ancient Egypt where the idea of human as co-creator with God is reflected in the

Egyptian symbolism of Osiris. In Egypt we gain vital knowledge about the Tree of Light and Serpent in the Garden and the means to stimulate the cosmic G-Spot.

3.

THE COSMIC G-SPOT STIMULATOR

In the Egyptian hall at the New York Metropolitan Museum of Art hangs the limestone fresco (next page) from the 3,300-year old chapel at Abydos that takes us to the heart of Egyptian Gnosis. In the relief we see Ramses I offering a tray of food, including grapes, and a floral offering to the massive Osiris symbol, which features the levitating serpent (or tone) and a head or pillar symbol that matches the Cathar symbols and . Beside the symbol of her husband stands the goddess Isis. The elaborate platform supporting the symbol resembles in form and I believe, function, the biblical Ark of the Covenant. This serpent has been called the spirit of the Oracle. It matches the wriggly serpent Leviathon, from whence came the *Levites*, the *Ophite* gurus of Moses and handlers of the Ark of the Covenant, and the healing or brazen serpent Nehushtan Moses was instructed to 'lift' or levi-tate.

This pillar, the Egyptians claimed, held the *head* and *soul* of Osiris, suggesting the serpent and head symbols are

interchangeable, as in the previous example of the Divine
Force. It *is* the Oracle that linked Heaven and Earth. A clue
to the object's function is provided by the hieroglyphics
that accompany it. They read *give, water, lord, life* and
powers. The emblem of Abydos, in fact of Gnosis, may be
studied here and in three dimensions in the graphic by the
artist Dana Augustine on the page following.

*The Osiris Symbol, Abydos. H. 44 in. Metropolitan Museum
of Art, New York. It is the model for the Cathar Cross.*

*The ABYDOS pillar superimposed on the human body, or the human **bodhi**, or enlightenment, tree.*

Abydos was the shrine where Osiris or O-Sar-Is ('the serpent of light or wisdom'), or the Osiris Symbol, which resembles a phallic stimulator, entered the 'underworld' waters of *Nun* (*none*, Zero) also called the 'Fish of Isis', his wife, and symbolized by the Vesica Piscis or 'fish' or 'vagina' symbol $\bigcirc$, and awakened the Divine Force.[1] Fish and womb were synonymous in the tradition of the Greek *oracle* at *Delphi*, named after *delphos* meaning both fish and womb. Isis was portrayed wearing a fish head and, like all gods, she held the key of life.

Isis was called *Abtu*, the Great Fish of the *Abyss*, the 'hole of the serpent'. Significantly, additional names for Abydos are *Abju* and *Abtu*, which was *Abz* or *Abyss*. Abz matches the Sumerian AB.ZU, 'Great Deep', from whence came the gods of the Sumerians riding upon serpent ships.

Stretching the term ABZ we find that, in English, Abz is *A Buzz*. In comic strips the buzz sound is symbolized by the $\mathcal{NV} \ \mathcal{NV} \ \mathcal{NV}$. As we have seen, this symbol speaks a thousand divine words. Just one drop of the essence it oozes Φ brings enlightenment.

From the sum of these definitions I propose now, and will further explain later, that Abydos was the place, the Oracle, where the buzz or tone of life came through. Operational, Isis's Pillar of Osiris was a sort of stimulator of the cosmic G-Spot that, like Athena's spear, lit up like a light house and fed the people a sensuous experience.

When the tube opened it took one on a ride like no other revealing new realms of experience.

THEY FOUND IT

The way these terms and symbols we have looked at dovetail makes it easy to connect the dots between the Mayan, Zoroastrian, Egyptian, Sumerian, as well as the Cathar traditions with that of the Gnostic Ophites who 'lifted' the serpent ladder to the Milky Way.

Shortly after 300 B.C., a god who displayed this symbolism was created in Alexandria, Egypt from two existing Greek and Egyptian gods. His purpose was to symbolize the synthesis of the two cultures that the new Greek rulers of Egypt hoped would occur. The new god's name was *Sarapis*.

The name Sarapis, says Godfrey Higgins, comes from *Soros*, the name given by the Egyptians to a *(s)tone coffin*, and *Apis* or *Opis*, the name given to Osiris.[2] These two words combined result in *Soro-Apis* or *Sara-Opis*, 'the tomb of the bull' or 'the tomb of the soul'.

Among the other meanings suggested for the word *Sarapis* are: 'The Soul of Osiris' and 'The Sacred Serpent'. Both meanings are descriptive of the Pillar of Osiris.

There once stood a statue of Sarapis in the famed *Sarapeum* of Alexandria. The Sarapeum was regarded as one of the wonders of the ancient world. It was named after an earlier famous Sarapeum which once stood in Memphis and which contained a library with over 300,000 volumes. Within the temple was an emerald statue of Saropis. He was usually shown *robed head to foot in heavy draperies*.

I suspect that he was heavily robed for the reason that, as shown here, he apparently had the body of a serpent.

Sar-Opis

Underneath the temple of Sar-Opis destroyed by the Romans was a labyrinth. There, says Manly P. Hall, *"were found strange mechanical contrivances by the priests in the subterranean crypts and caverns where the nocturnal initiatory rites were celebrated."*[3] After passing through the ordeals presented by these machines, the initiates found themselves face to face with Sarapis.

What were these strange "mechanical contrivances?" They obviously functioned as an oracle. Could one of them have been the Pillar of Osiris that revealed the serpent-deity that 'lived' in the Pillar? I shall have more to say on this later. For now, let us continue our survey of the Ophite background of the Gnostic teaching.

The Gnostic Fathers Basilides (c. 125 A.D.) and Valentinus (mid 2nd century) introduced the Ophite Milky Way and serpent symbolism into Christianity. Both took advantage of the magnificent libraries of Alexandria, the product of an affluent trading center of interchange of religious ideas and as the intellectual meeting point between Egyptian, Buddhist, Jewish and Greek thought. I'm of the opinion that they knew the secrets of the Pillar of Osiris.

It is important to remember that Alexandria was home to another of the Seven Wonders of the ancient world, the *Pharos* (Pharaoh) Lighthouse ⊙ of Alexandria. Ancient accounts such as those by Strabo and Pliny the Elder give us a brief description of this remarkable 40 story "tower" and the magnificent white marble cover. They tell us how the mysterious mirror could reflect the light 35 miles away.

Legend says the mirror was also used to detect and burn enemy ships before they could reach the shore.

In my view, the Pharos lighthouse was a tribute to the Pillar of Light, the pillar of the Oracle, which also stood approximately 40 stories tall. It spawned the modern day lighthouse, the beacon for ships at sea.

In contrast to other religions, Gnostic Christianity first appeared in Alexandria not as a religious sect or school but as an attitude accepted by enlightened pagans and Jews.

These Gnostics viewed Jesus as a divine man, an Oracle, and as a target to be emulated. As shown on the next page, Jesus lifted the mouth of the serpent and showed the way to activate a cosmic potential within everyone through Gnosis. This knowledge was not written down, but rather, was passed orally and symbolically by the Oracle. The disciple obtained his knowledge through initiation into the Spiritual Mysteries. The teachings were presented to him in the form of symbols (the universal Language of the Gods), and his knowledge of religion and philosophy depended upon his understanding of symbolism. The Oracle *breathed* the ultimate knowledge upon the pupil.

Jesus lifts or opens the mouth of the Leviathon (wormhole) with the 'Cross', actually a symbol for the Pillar of Osiris. In so doing, he models the story of Mose, Isis and Athena.

In Gnostic teaching Jesus emerges as composite 'salvation hero' who possessed intimate details of the sacred science of antiquity, (which I propose centered on the ⚕), that fused art, science, philosophy and religion (particularly Egyptian and Sumerian) into an experience of cosmic proportions that awakened the soul.

This sacred science was a science of the soul. (The master alchemist Schwaller de Lubicz, one of the major thinkers of the twentieth century, helped bring this science to light in the 20th century.) Interestingly, the Hebrew word *nahash* means 'serpent'. A related word *nephesh* means 'soul'. In this way the word-symbols serpent and soul are interchangeable. The Egyptian glyph ⚕ , along with all of the serpent symbolism we have examined, can, therefore, symbolize the science of the soul. When Jesus 'slays' the serpent Leviathon (the Milky Way), as he will do in the 'End Times', it may mean he will 'lift' and release the secret essence ♈, ♀ of the Milky Way's cosmic G-spot.

Some may protest that Jesus was never called a serpent and should, therefore, not be associated with this symbolism. I have followed a fascinating network of connections that show that he was indeed connected with the serpents of wisdom, the Druids. According to *Strong's Concordance*, the word the Bible uses to describe Jesus is *adder*, an adjective used in Ezekiel 17:8 that implies *"noble and majestic.*[4]*"* It is the same as *addir* "mighty, majestic", which describes God's majestic *holiness* which was demonstrated by His delivering Israel from Egyptian bondage. The word is applied to the Messiah, the Mighty Man, which is why Jesus is portrayed receiving the transmission of the Cloak of the Mighty Man.

Two less frequently occurring nouns are '*adderet* and '*eder*'. *Strong's* says *adderet* may be "luxurious outer garment, mantle, cloak," Genesis 25:25. *Eder* may refer to a "luxurious outer garment."[5]

A phonetically similar word *addir* means 'serpent' in Ireland. The Druids used this term to describe a wise man. Numerous authors, including Gordon Strachan, have shown the many important Druid connections in Jesus' life and teaching.[6] A number of legends suggest that Jesus traveled to the British Isles with Joseph of Arimathea. The Druids have been shown by many authors to be teachers of Gnosis. It is therefore reasonable to conclude that the title adder would have been applied to Jesus. Now we can understand, he is called so because he wore the adderet cloak or garment of light.

In 140 AD Valentinus went to Rome in a doomed attempt to become Bishop of Rome and lead the Church along Gnostic lines. At the time his followers had been engaged in a life and death struggle with the Church of Rome, whose leaders were often obsessed with the possible threat Alexandria presented to their power.

Irenaeus, Bishop of Lyon, France, who formulated early orthodox Catholic Church rules, and attacked Gnosticism as arch heresy met Valentinus's effort with a fierce rebuttal.

In addition to the reasons previously cited, the primary reason was because the Gnostics denied that Christ appeared in the flesh (instead Christ is a *flash*, tone or vibration embodied by Jesus) and they urged people to seek direct access to God unmediated by church or clergy and to become as God. *Oracle* is the term used throughout history for one who has direct access to God.

Within two centuries the Gnostic books would be banned as "heretical". The libraries of Alexandria would be burned before the fourth century.

The only evidence of Gnostic Christianity's existence was the denunciations by the Church, its enemy. That is, until the light reappeared when two peasants discovered the Nag Hammadi library by 'accident' in 1945, shortly after the sacrifice of millions of lives during the holocaust of WW II.

The *Gospel of Thomas*, one of the Gnostic texts found preserved in the Nag Hammadi Library, and recorded by Jesus' *twin*, Iudas or Judas Thomas, begins with the statement:

'Whosoever discovers the interpretation of these sayings will not taste death.'

Thomas gives these words of the living Jesus:

Jesus said, 'I am not your master. Because you have drunk, you have become drunk from the bubbling stream which I have measured out....

He who will drink from my mouth will become as I am: I myself shall become he, and the things that are hidden will be revealed to him.'

He who will drink from my mouth will become as I am. I shall bcome he.

This is the essence of the Gnostic heresy. Simply, it says Jesus taught the secret of the serpent of Divine Force.

When we drink from this Divine Force   spit from his

mouth   , which, we know now, is the Milky Way, we become a Christ. This is why the Orthodox Church despises this gospel. It not only contains the actual words of the living Jesus that promises that anyone can become Christ, rather than the compiled and distilled words created by church, but also it suggests Jesus is the serpent of Eden.

In the *Gospel of Thomas* Jesus says:

> I am the light that is over all things.
> I am all:
> All come forth from me,
> And all attained to me.
> *Split the wood,*
> *And I am there,*
> *Lift a stone,*
> *And you will find me there.*[8]

As all Grail questers learn, the center of the Milky Way

is the Grail. Once the Grail Stone or (s)Tone of God is 'lifted' (understood or stolen) or stimulated, the quester discovers this Stone is inscribed (a buzz) with a mystery teaching, which reveals the solutions to the riddles or secrets of creation and enables one to control the elements, and, voila, to become an Oracle.

Following this linguistic path we note that the Greek word for (s)tone is *Cephas* or *Kephas*. Kephas is from *Kephalos*, meaning *head*. The Knights Templar and alchemists referred to this keystone as the *dead head* and symbolized it by a ⊙ (the Cathar serpent ☿ when viewed from the face or head on). Cephas is the original name for St. Peter (from *petros*, meaning 'rock'), the Galilean fisherman who became Jesus' chief disciple and the Head of the Catholic Church. By this interpretation, the Oracle Stone is the Head of the Church. To Gnostic Christians, Christ, not Peter, is the head of the Church. This was not a man, as the Church portrayed Peter. It was a teaching, a science ⚲ , that transcended humankind.

Lifting the head or stone enabled us to 'split the wood', or rather, *spit* the Wood ☿ . Like the stone, Jesus is using the wood as a symbol for something else. That something else is the Word, the sacred life force energy upon which the world is built.

Professor Helmut Koester of Harvard University notes that though ultimately the alchemical *Gospel of Thomas* was condemned and destroyed by the evolving orthodox church, *it may be as old or older than the four canonical gospels preserved, and* even have *served as a source document to them.*[9]

Dr. Stephan Hoeller explains that these Gnostic Christians held a "conviction that direct, personal and absolute knowledge of the authentic truths of existence is accessible to human beings, and, moreover, that the attainment of such knowledge must always constitute the supreme achievement of human life."[10] Comprehending the secrets of the Pillar of Osiris, I propose, enabled them to make this connection.

No wonder Ireneaus attacked the Gnostics and classified their teachings as heretical: if people participated in such a religion, they would be in an orgasmic state of ecstacy and would be their own Saviors. They would have no need for his church and its demonization of the human body! Worse even yet, Irenaeus was particularly dismayed that many "foolish" (his word) women especially were attracted to the heretical teachings. Gnostics claimed to receive secret teaching from prophets named Mary Magdalene, Salome and Martha. Among them men and women were considered equal. One of the early Gnostic Gospels discovered at Nag Hammadi was the *Gospel of Mary*. By slamming the door in the face of women, the Church not only rejected the teaching of Jesus, whose intimate disciple was Mary Magdalene, but also set back social evolution by a couple thousand years.

Interestingly, the Nag Hammadi has the following to say about Mary in the "Gospel of Philip":

The companion of the Savior is Mary Magdalene. (But Jesus loved) here more than the other disciples and used to kiss her (often) on her (mouth). The rest of (the disciples were offended by it). They said to him, "Why do you love her more than all of us?" The Savior answered and said to them, "Why do I not love you as (I love) her?

The "Dialogue of the Savior" (another Gnostic gospel) not only includes Mary Magdalene as one of the three disciples chosen to receive special (secret) teachings but also uplifts her above the other two, Thomas and Matthew: *"she spoke as the woman who knew all."*

Cross-checking Egyptian mythology, we discover an astonishing Egyptian description of *'the All'*.

The side posts of Egyptian temple's entrance doors are often ornamented with horizontal bands of bas-reliefs portraying the three symbols:

Uas -- the tree branch, commonly called the 'Key of the Nile',

TET or Djed (center) -- the Pillar of Osiris, and

Ankh -- 'life'.

Uas   Djed   Ankh   *Uas   Ankh   Uas*

59

These three symbols are placed on a basket. This basket is *the All*. What Mari Magdalane appears to have known is the secrets of a collection of four Power Tools, and ultimately, the secrets of the , the Stimulator of the Cosmic G-Spot that produces the *oil* ('all' with a Tennessee accent) of life. Revelation of these secrets increases the enjoyment of our lives tremendously. To the controlling religious authorities this is heresy. Of all the Popes not one has probably ever discovered the cosmic G-Spot. Ignorance of it has caused untold misery.

4.

THE REALITY OF THE RULERS

The Soul, the soul speaks:
Who cast me into the Tibil, the earth,
Who cast me into the Tibil, the earth,
who chained me in the wall?
Who cast me into the stocks,
*which matches **the fullness** of the world?*
Who threw a chain round me,
that is without measure?
Who clothed me in a coat
of all colors and kinds?

The Soul in Its Coat of All Colors.
From the Mandaean *Ginza*.

Theodotus, a Gnostic teacher writing in Asia Minor
between A.D. 140 and 160, explained that the sacred
strength of Gnosis reveals *"who we were, what we have
become, where we have been **cast** out of, where we are
bound for, what we have been purified of, what generation
and regeneration are."*
Who are we? What have we become? Where have we
been *cast (made, formed, shed, warped, twisted, vomited,*

61

dropped, projected, thrown like a stone) out of? What have we been purified of? What is generation and regeneration?

The central text of Christian Gnosticism (which, as we have seen, is a collection of ideas, not a religion) that answers these questions is the *Hypostasis of the Archons* ("Reality of the Rulers").[1] Written in the third century, this anonymous tract presented an esoteric interpretation of Genesis 1-6 (which chronicled the Hebrew version of the Sumerian creation myth of man by the Anunnaki) partially in the form of a revelatory conversation between an angel and a questioner (probably an Oracle). It recounts the Gnostic myth from the creation of a figure named *Yaldabaoth* (who created humanity) down to Noah and the flood and concludes with a prediction of the final advent of the savior, the destruction of demonic powers and the victory of the Gnostic children of light over the children of darkness. By extension it predicts a world in which everyone becomes an Oracle and experiences the ultimate love and knowledge. In other words, it predicts a period of Peace on Earth and a return of the golden camel arches of love ⌣⌣⌣.

As the title suggests this work proclaims the reality of the *Archonic* rulers, an enslaving authority of lesser gods that *rings* the Earth and whom the Gnostics, the children of the (blue) light, believe they are in conflict with and must overcome in order to create Peace and return to the Source

or God Head

The main characters in the mythological drama presented in this remarkable text are the 'blind' ruler *Samael*, also called *Yaldabaoth* and *Sakla* ("fool"), who creates the Archons and with them a big mess; Sophia, who created Samael as her consort, who has to come down from heaven to outwit the rulers to clean up her own even bigger mess; the Serpent, the Instructor, the Oracle, who advises Adam and Eve to eat the (blue) fruit forbidden by the Archons; and *Norea* ('light of E.A.'), the daughter of Eve, a pure ('Cathar') virgin who knows the secrets of the Oracle.

Another Gnostic text included in the Nag Hammadi cache that relates in detail this soul vs. rulers drama is *The Apocryphon of John*, translated by Frederik Wisse.[2] These secret words that the resurrected Jesus taught to his disciple

John also explains the God Head   , the creation and fall story told in Genesis, as well as the means by which humanity could achieve salvation. As in the *Hypostasis*, Yahweh, the creator of Genesis, is portrayed as an anti-Divine being.

According to this text, before the material world came into existence, there was the Light, described as a Trinity

,   . From this Light came a series of *Em*anations, various cosmic beings in male-female pairs called *Aeons*. The fall occurs when one of these Emanations, Sophia, decides to make a copy of herself (from thought) for her consort without her other male half, and without the approval of the Great Spirit. Consequently, she misfires and produces the lion-faced serpent creator-god *Yaldabaoth*. This is the twisted serpent of wisdom the Gnostics called *Chnoubis* (from the Egyptian *kneph*, the Father of Ptah). Another way of spelling *Chnoubis* is *Kanobis* (the name of the Essenes) and *Knoubis* or *Cannabis*. He is the *canna* (serpent, conduit) *bis* or *buzz* from *anna*, heaven.

*Gnostic gem showing the lion headed serpent
Yaldabaoth, also called Chnoubis.*

The lion-headed Chnoubis is the same as the Zervan Akaran, *boundless* time, *of the Mithraic mysteries, symbolized as a lion-headed man enwrapped by six coils of the serpent who head completes the seventh turn. Four wings sprout from his back symbolizing the four elements. On his chest he wears the lightning bolt of illumination, visibly manifest in the bodies of the enlightened.*

65

Another Nag Hammadi text, *On the Origin of the World* compares the birth of Chnoubis to an aborted fetus since there was no spirit ('Divine Particle') or other half in it.[3] Sophia was disturbed by her defective creation, her heir she thought an error. It rushed to her. She turned to it and *blew into its face* in the *Abyss*.

Or, the A Buzz 〜 〜 〜

Sophia's breathing procedure is duplicated by Jesus in John 20:22...*He (Jesus) breathed on them, and said to them, "Receive the Holy Spirit" (Sophia).*

The aborted creature is sent to rule over matter (below the heavens). From the Abyss the creature arose, ignorant of how he had come into being. (Among early peoples, says Harold Bayley, it is believed that Earth and Sky were once wedded, but that long ago something – in some cases a snake – cut them asunder.)[4]

When Sophia saw him moving about in the depths of the waters (of the Abyss) she said to him, "*Child, pass through to here,*" whose equivalent is "*yalda baoth.*"

According to *On The Origin of the World*, this poignant statement was the beginning of language and verbal communications between the gods, angels and mankind. At that moment, we can surmise, all symbols, the Language of the Gods, were downloaded to Yaldabaoth. This, I believe, is the symbol system of the Cathars.

The result of this communication was the creation of humanity by Yaldabaoth. When the lion-headed serpent saw that it was only himself he concluded that he was alone in the universe. From matter he made himself an abode and he called it heaven. And from matter he made a footstool, and he called it Earth. (These are the footprints in the sand we must *fill*.) He then created humanity to populate the Earth.

It is important to remember that Yaldabaoth is ignorant of the Divine Particle of Sophia blown into his face. When he looked up at Sophia talking to him he did not see her face, rather *he saw in the water* ∿ *the likeness of himself* -- ∿ . And because of that voice, he called himself Yaldabaoth, *Child, pass through* ◯ *to here*.

The heaven created by Yaldabaoth appears to be a version of the *Abyss* known as the *Abtu*, the abode of the four corners bordered by the lion, bull, man and eagle. This four-cornered cosmic water world (the *Looking Glass* I term *Aquaria*, the cosmic aquarium) matches the four-cornered Sea of Glass, the throne of Christ described in the Book of Revelation. The Abtu was the "mansion" of God whose four outer walls are made of stone, whose foundation is sand (silicon), its exterior jasper, is the crystal Christ's court is composed of in the Book of Revelation.[5] As seen by John the Revelator, it is 'full of eyes" (*stars, consciousness*). It is hidden, unknown, invisible, nothing save the solar disk sees it.[6] This is because it is a floating crystalline cube, a Sea of Glass, a cloaked container of life mirroring the blackness of space.

Yaldabaoth is trapped in some sort of mirror world, cosmic aquarium or glass Pandora's Box. In calling to him to pass through to here, Sophia (who, recall is Isis and

Athena) was trying to coax Yaldabaoth out of the aquarium and to return to the Pleroma.

The Griffon atop the winged globe draws the Sea of Glass or the Ark of the Christos.

In *Ark of the Christos* I described this Sea of Glass as a container and, based upon the latest science, as a wormhole or cosmic transportation device.[7] It functions as a *babel* or 'gate' to God.

Interestingly, the Greek word for confusion (babel) is *Gryphe* (*grief*), which is the root of Gryphon or Griffon, a mythical creature that is a hybrid of the lion (Earth) and eagle (Sky).[8] Jesus is called the Master-Griffon because as God and man he represents the union of the divine and the human. In fairy tales the Griffin, the Bird of Gold, figures prominently as a *transporter* through the golden gate or the conduit ∿.[9] Herodotus regarded the Griffin as the guardian of god's treasures, and on a higher plane, the way or door of salvation, the Sea of Glass. A description of Sky Man or Griffon-Gate Man in his cloak of linen is found in Daniel 10:4-7.

The four Cosmic Forces that compose the Sea of Glass are represented by the Sphinx, the guardian of the hall of life that is a composite creature of the lion, bull, man and eagle. These are the four creatures seen by the Oracle Ezekiel and, I believe, symbolize the four Power Tools of the All. They symbolize the four elements of which Yaldabaoth ⋀⋁ is a master of transmutation. By rearranging these elements the ⋀⋁ transforms into the air we breathe, the landscape we see and the entire ecosystem of which we are a part. To paraphrase Jeremy Narby's description of DNA (composed of the four biochemical elements or bases A,C,T,G arranged in 64 codons) it has transformed and multiplied itself into an incalculable number of species, while remaining exactly the same.[10] Arranged in three dimensions of height, depth, width (plus time) they form a *cube*.

The four bases are paired on the DNA molecule, and in a very specific way: A always with T and G always with C. Connecting the base pairs are alternating sugar and phosphate units, forming a structure that resembles a ladder. The ladder is actually three-dimensional, though; it takes the form of two strands twisted into a long spiral -- the famous "double helix."

How is it that this molecule consisting of only six basic components (four bases, a phosphate, and a sugar) can contain all the information required to make almost a million types of animals and nearly a half-million species of plants?

The Gnostics have answered this for us. It is, in a manner of speaking, a language, a language of life. DNA is capable of speaking anything into existence.

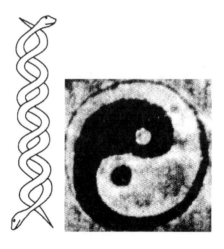

The DNA double helix and the Yin Yang symbol for the Androgyne. "The double helix represented as a pair of snakes. By turning the picture upside down, you can see that the molecule is completely symmetrical – each half of the double helix can serve as a template for the synthesis of its complementary half."[11]

The DNA comparison is apropos here as, next, recounts the *On the Origin of the World*, Yaldabaoth *opened his mouth* and he created an androgyne, a bisexual being (a combination of the feminine oval or egg and the masculine triangle) that combined the male and female. He cooed at his offspring and when his eyes opened, he looked at his father, and he said to him, "Eee!" Then his father called him Eee-a-o (E.A.O. or Yao). He created six more androgynes for a total of *seven*.

As the lion, bull, man and eagle are symbolic of the four Cosmic Forces, these seven androgynes created by Yaldabaoth are symbolic of the seven sacred forces of: the seven heavens; the seven divine entities of Zoroastrianism; the seven-headed serpent that bit the Buddha while in the river of initiation; and the seven Anunnaki of Sumerian mythology. They are not yet "people," human or otherwise. The Anunnaki sages or "gods" (variously numbered as 7, 50 and 900), in general, represent the seven "nether spheres" (or *neter*, Egyptian for 'god' spheres) and guardians of the seven "nodes," "notes" or "gates" through which the "sun of God" passes into the netherworld or darkness (the world outside the Sea of Glass). (For more on the Anunnaki connection to the Sea of Glass, please see my book *Ark of the Christos*.)

The seven-fold knowledge or wisdom is found in the seven *liberal arts*, the seven bodies of knowledge that liberate the mind and create a "liber or free man," one who is not a slave. They were divided into the three-fold **Trivium** of Grammar, Logic, and Rhetoric, and the fourfold **Quadrivium** of Arithmetic, Geometry, Music, and Astronomy. These words mean, respectively, a three-way and a four-way **crossroads**, implying that these paths of knowledge are fundamentally interconnected. By studying the links and intersections among these disciplines, one learns to recognize analogies, patterns, correspondences, through which the archetypal ideas that underlie and unite the cosmos manifest themselves in the world of time and space.[12]

Let us add to this list of 'sevens', as does Schwaller de Lubicz, the seven fundamental constants: e, charge of the electron; m, mass of the electron; M, mass of the proton; h, Planck's constant; c, speed of light; g, constant of gravitation; and the constant constant.[13] They are the seven "stars" in the hand of Jesus in the Book of Revelation.

The Mayans taught that the Milky Way gave us seven powers called $k'ul$. They are distributed in our bodies.[14] The Mayans mastered these sacred powers to become Quetzalcoatl or Kukulkan. *Kan* or *can* is Mayan word for "serpent" and "four" and alludes to the highest esoteric knowledge of the Maya.[15]

The Oracles of the mystery schools were taught that they could transform and expand their awareness through seven thresholds of consciousness or *chakras*.

It is important to note that the chakras are considered an inner ladder to Heaven. This precisely matches the image used by traditional shamans to discuss the creation of life. The serpent, the rope, the vine, the ladder or stairway to heaven of celestial origin are interchangeable.

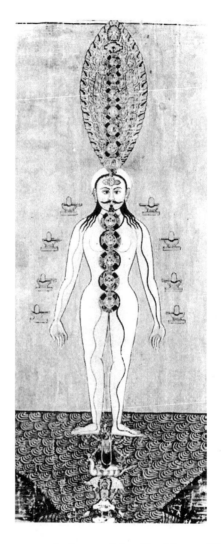

The seven chakras of the 'Ladder to Heaven'.

Mircea Eliade has shown that these symbols are also the *axis mundi*, or axis of the world called MERU, and symbolized by the Pillar of Osiris, the cosmic G-Spot Stimulator.[16] According to Eliade, the Meru pillar gives access to the Otherworld and to shamanic knowledge, and a serpent or dragon often guards this passage (along with the *Language of the Birds*). In Egypt this pillar-serpent combination was featured in the hieroglyph of Osiris

. Lifting the serpent, i.e. mastering each of the four Cosmic Forces represents the way to *pass through, dive,*

to here, to pass through the Sea of Glass and return to the land of Sophia.

ENTER SOPHIA

The *Hypostasis of the Archons* tells us that Yaldabaoth

created 365 archonic angels to rule over the Earth and aid in the creation of man; man himself is *fashioned after the perfect Father's image* (the four forces), *who was mirrored on the water* . This creation was lifeless for a long time. It did not buzz, humm or contain the ring

of life.

This is when Sophia decided she wanted to retrieve the Divine Particle, the power she had given to Yaladabaoth (a fact to which he was ignorant) when she *blew* (blue) *in his face.* She sends *five lights* to visit Yaladabaoth who advise him that the power of the mother, the Divine Particle, should be awakened in man. And they said to Yaldabaoth *'blow into his face'* something *of your spirit and his body will arise.* And Yaldabaoth blew into man's face the spirit, and the power of his mother (which is the Divine Particle)

♏, ♀ went out of his mouth and into the body of the man; whereupon the man becomes luminous by virtue of the Divine Particle. Now, the man is buzzing.

In that moment the rest of the archons became jealous, because though they had a hand in creating man, his intelligence, vis-a-vis the Divine Particle, was greater than that of those who had made him.

So commences a perpetual struggle between the forces of darkness and the force of light for the Divine Particles (Blue Apples) in man that continues to this very day.

The *Hypostasis of the Archons* says the evil archons clothed man in a material body, a casket or tomb (a Saropis). They contrived to keep Adam and Eve, along with their Divine Particles -- and Sophia herself -- trapped in matter, enslaved forever in the wheel of reincarnation as tillers of the Garden of Eden. In this way humans provide food for the rulers (more on this subject momentarily).

The *Hypostasis* also describes a veil that exists between the world above and the realms below. "And the shadow came into being beneath the veil; and that shadow became matter; and that shadow was projected apart."

With the application of the veil thus began a program of mind-body control-- or soul enslavement -- maintained by Yaldabaoth's Archons (rulers) which involved keeping mankind distracted by material problems and concerns, imprisoned by its own fear of death, of mortality, and ignorant of its true, divine nature.

Hence the soul became "entangled in the darkness of matter," confined to bodily identification, ruled by a Church and condemned to endless, repeated reincarnation (or reincarceration), without possibility of parole, of graduation to goldhood or godliness.

The Gnostics believed that the soul on its way back to the *Pleroma* would have to pass through Yaldabaoth. To escape, said the Gnostics, we must awaken the Divine Particle that enables the *child to pass through to here* and return to Sophia in a realm called the *Pleroma* ('fullness').

Along the way, Archons waiting at each of the seven heavens would also have to be passed. In order to pass these beings, the soul needed to give a password. The Egyptians held a similar view.

In the designs shown her from Egypt and Europe, the little souls emerge jubilantly from the mouth of a Serpent (or worm hole). As Harold Bayley notes, these designs express the passage "Osiris enters the tail of a great serpent, was drawn through its body and came out through its mouth, and was then born anew."[17] The story of Jesus/Jonah and the whale mirrors this story.

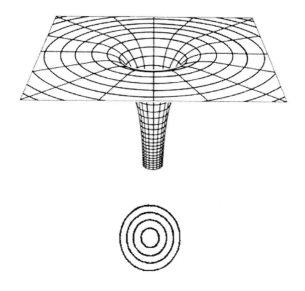

A depiction of a wormhole from the side and top.

The passage through the 'wheel or whirl of life' is modeled by Ixion, whose name is akin to axis. *His death took place at the hub of the universe, the axis, which later became the cross of Christ.*

The Cathar symbolism returns us to Athena, the goddess of the serpent born. Jason/Jesus, 'the serpent born', and Athena (Sophia). The soul 'passes through to here' (Pleroma).

Today, we call the seven heavens *Hyperspace*, a plane where *time* and *space* does not exist, and all events happen *synchronistically* or at the same time. It is the area beyond the astral plane, and between all physical realities. The astral plane is the border zone between hyperspace and the physical world. This dimension is considered very dangerous, as it is the realm of disincarnates as well as other other terrestrial beings. Travelers to Hyperspace report that the waters are filled with symbols and hieroglyphs that glow in psychedelic colors. Information pulses through one's entire being. For a shining moment, you experience *all pervading knowing*. You have patched through to the Source, Sophia. You are an Oracle.

The *way through* is called a wormhole, a cosmic transportation system that is the hallmark of Type II ('Star Trek-type') civilizations according to a scheme for classifying advanced technological civilizations proposed by Nikolai Kardashev in 1964 and adopted by Dr. Michio Kaku.[18] He identified three possible civilization types and distinguished between them in terms of the power they could muster for the purposes of interstellar communications. A Type I civilization would be able to marshal energy resources for communications an a planet-wide scale, equivalent to the entire present power consumption of the human race. A Type II civilization would surpass this by a factor of approximately ten billion, by exploiting the total energy output of its central star. Finally, a Type III civilization would have evolved far enough to tap the energy resources of an entire galaxy.

⊙ is a representation of a top down view of our Milky Way galaxy with the ● representing its Central Sun or Galactic Core, called *Tula*.

The Milky Way in Infrared
Credit: E. L. Wright (UCLA), The COBE Project, DIRBE, NASA

Our's is a disk-shaped galaxy ⊙ whose central nuclear bulge is a star nursery, a fact reflected in the symbol used by the Alchemists who alternated between and when signifying the *essence of a substance*, or the *spirit*.[19]

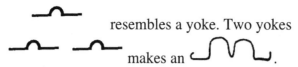

resembles a yoke. Two yokes makes an .

As we can see from this symbolism, the alchemists appear to have approached their craft from the perspectives exemplified more by a Type II than a Type I civilization. I suspect they utilized the energy of the G-Spot.

EPINOIA

In *Hypostasis of the Archons*, the blessed One, the Mother-Father, the beneficent and merciful One, sends a helper to Adam to help wake him up. She is the luminous *Epinoia*, which is hidden in Adam, but comes out of him, who is called Life (and Sophia). "And she assists him by restoring him to his *fullness* and by teaching him about the descent of his seed (and) by *teaching him about the way of ascent.*"

She is the Oracle "who was to awaken his thinking." And patch him into the means to return him to *Pleroma*, '*full*ness'. The pun on *fool* and *full* does not go unnoticed. As in the Tarot, the Fool symbolizes the seeker on a quest to find the inner Magician or Oracle.

In a tale reminiscent of the creation of Eve, the chief archon took a part of Adam and he made a woman in the likeness of Epinoia which had appeared to him. And Adam saw the woman beside him. And in that moment the luminous Epinoia appeared, and she lifted the veil, which lay over his mind. She awakened his, and later, Eve's thinking.

81

In *The Apochryphan of John*, it is Christ or Krist, "the re-membrance of the **Pleroma**" (the re-memberer or 'patcher'), who patches into the prison-planet of Earth (ala Neo patching into the Matrix) to remind humanity of its heavenly origins. Christ could not enter in the flesh, said the Cathars, but could become it. Only those who possess this *gnios* (from the Hebrew IO, 'wisdom') or *Gnosis* or knowledge and have lived ascetic lives can put on the blue light robe of Krist and cross into hyperspace, the realm of light.[20]

Here, an examination of Epinoia's name is helpful. Without the vowels Epinoia is simply *PN*. Add an 'a' and we have *Pan*, meaning 'bread', 'manna', 'dew', 'wisdom'. Words commencing with PN include *pneuma* (from German *pnein*, to breathe), meaning *soul; spirit; the breath of life*. In Christian theology *pneuma* is the Holy Spirit. *Pneumatic* means *of or containing wind, air or gases: opposed to dense or solid*. In philosophy or theology it is *the doctrine of spiritual substances*.

I find it most synchronistic that the word *Epinoia* is so close to *Epona*, the Celtic Horse goddess or White Mare. The English *Mare* is the French *mere*, meaning *Mother*. In Latin *mare* means sea (a pun on *see*). In ancient Egypt *mer* meant *to love*.[21] In French, *AMOR* means love, and is the name of the religion of the Cathars. AMOR was opposed by ROMA or AMOR in reverse.

Ma Re is the Ma or Mother Re or *Ray* of *Love* that helps us to see beyond the power of Roma into the Pleroma, the land of Peace. Mare (Mari and Mary) is the

82

'horse' (also called an Ark or Arch) that enables the shaman to fly through the air, to reach the Pleroma. This may explain why Christ rides a White Horse in Revelation.

"Behold a White Horse (ray or wave $\bigwedge\!\!\bigwedge$), and he that rode him was called faithful and true (blue)".

The mare, Al Barak, ridden by Muhammed is another example of this symbolism.

When we sum the puns, this particular book of the *Nag* (or *Horse*) Hammadi scrolls contains the secret of the key of life, the *Epinoia* that contains the Holy Spirit.

In Egypt, the key that, once breathed, delivered the Holy Spirit was called the *ankh* or Key of Life and was part of a collection four Power Tools. It is demonstrated on the next page by Akhenaton, the 'Heretic King', whose religion of ATON highly influenced the Gnostic Christians.

In depictions from his city of Amarna Akhenaton possessed the rod or wand of miracle, the Key of Life, through which he channeled the Keys of Life to Earth as described in the Gnostic Apocryphon of John.

The hand delivers the three-fold symbol for 'mist', which is interchangeable with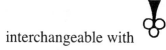

Taking a cue from the Egyptians, the Gnostic Christians combined the masculine and phallic **+** symbol of the four Cosmic Forces with the feminine ○, or oval, the gate, to form the Key of Life, the symbol for the coveted esoteric principles of *G*eneration, i.e. the secret of becoming an Oracle.

Without the Key, the Earth, said the Gnostics, was a prison-planet ruled by the negative aspect of Yaldabaoth. The soul would continue to reincarnate repeatedly until the power of Yaldabaoth and his evil angels (the "archons" which encircle the earth) could be broken.

2nd Century Coptic or Egyptian –Christian ankhs.

The children of the light are the "awakened ones," the Type II Illuminati, who have discovered the secret of their creation, and opened the gate ⬭ or mouth of the serpent Yaldabaoth, the Milky Way, and *passed through* to the other side. The Gnostic's 'contest' is not against flesh and blood; rather against Yaldabaoth and the spirits of wickedness (the Archons).

With the Key of Life or Word of God vibrating, reverberating and buzzing through our veins/vines the atoms and molecules that make up our body become supercharged. We put on the miracle skin or Cloak of the

Illuminati. A person is transformed from homo sapien sapien to blue-blooded *homo maximus*, the Oracle, who radiates or rings of the force field described by Fulcanelli. This enabled one to rise or ascend from Earth.

Dr. Charles Muses, a mathematician, philosopher and computer scientist, who died in 2000, claims in his 1985 book *The Lion Path*, that the Egyptians had developed a technology in which tones, lights, and an as-yet unidentified plant are used, to "open a rusty valve", or trigger the production of large pulses of hormones similar to the ecdysone (ecdydsterone), produced by *larval* forms of insects, which allows the adult form to emerge.[22] In this way, they would allow the gestation or mutation of a *non-molecular body* – a new skin -- that would allow the survival of consciousness beyond physical death. Just as every chrysalis has embossed wings on it, wrote Muses, so too, does every mummy case have folded wings on it (as we will examine in the Abydos symbol later). *Larva* means 'a ghost' or 'specter'. It is the earliest stage of insect development, after it is hatched and before it is changed into a *chrysalis* or *pupa*, the stage in between the larval and adult forms.

These sacred tones (the Holy Grail) are used to allow us to shift through the veil of creation into the realm of pure unity of matter and energy. Traditional shamanic peoples around the world say the Blue Stone or Apple is actually how our soul travels to the inner realm and it is inside of a *quantum egg* or in an *"interphasic state of existence"* (able to jump through time and cross great distances or even to use this skill locally).

A preliminary stage between the human body and this non-molecular body was what I term the Cloak of the Illuminati, which is the Garment of the Oracle found in the example of the *Pallium* conferred upon or transmitted to Elisha by Elijah just before he *rose* into the heavens in a "whirlwind", *c.* 800 B.C.

In Egypt, Akhenaton's Disk worshippers of ATON (or ATEN) symbolized the ideogram for the word '*rise*' or '*to beam*' is three rays or beams of light falling from a disk.

As Muses points out, in this drawing *from the tomb of Tutankhamun* (Akhenaton's successor) on the next page we see the *three rays* or *beams* of Star-Power energy entering the forehead of the pupal Osiris. The word *sba*, ✳ "star" also means "door" and, with the determinative ⌂ for "walking," it meant "passing through a star-door," said Muses.[23] The *ba* or winged soul shown under this glyph in the figure indicates that it was the soul's passage through these doors that effected the Osirian transformation or metamorphosis into the immortal state and its glorified body.

We know that a sound can cause a human to enter a state of bliss or stupidity. Those who donned the Cloak knew the secret of the pitch or frequency of God that transmuted an ordinary human into a star walker. In the next chapter we will explore this idea in detail.

Osiris from the Second Shrine of Tutankhamun.

It is my contention that the supercloak in development at MIT is a prototype for a 21st century version of this cloak. As stated in the introduction, through a convergence of the four Power Tools – genes, bits, neurons and atoms --

we are creating a second skin for humanity. This effort is, ultimately, doomed to fail unless the fifth essence, *spirit*, is added. This essence was the core subject of the Gnostic mysteries.

We shall examine the Gnostic mysteries of this Cloak in the next chapter.

5.

THE HYMN OF THE PEARL

In a phenomenal Gnostic text the recovery of the Divine Particle (the Blue Apple) and the Cloak of Light is attributed to Jesus' twin brother Judas (*I-udas*) Thomas. *The Hymn of the Pearl* (= *HOP*) *or The Hymn of Judas Thomas and the Apostle in the Country of the Indians*, sometimes called *The Robe of Glory*, is a "spy" story.[1] It tells of Thomas's mission to Egypt or Al-Khema, the 'black' or 'hidden' land of alchemy to retrieve the Pearl/Soul. It is his autobiographical reminiscence of his soul's descent or entry into bodily incarnation and its eventual ascension from the body to the realm of peace. Thomas rises after he has acquired a garment as a reward for conquering the dragon of Egypt and stealing its Pearl. His story is a masculine version of Is-Tara's descent into the underworld to rescue her son-lover *Tammuz* (Thomas). The texts relating to this journey describe in detail the seven objects, including the *Pala Garment* ("ruler's garment") and blue stones, that Is-Tara put on before the start of her voyage.[2]

According to Bentley Layton's commentary in *The Gnostic Scriptures*, Thomas's putting on the supernatural garment (I call the Cloak of the Illuminati), is the beginning clue to unraveling the Gnostic mystery of salvation.[3] Beginning here and working backwards through the myth the ancient reader, the Fool, would pick up the secrets of self-knowledge that led them to the Oracle and Fullness (Pleroma). For this reason, says Layton, *HOP* has been identified with a special type of material called the "Gnostic call".[4] As we will see as we recount it in detail now, to understand this myth one would have needed familiarity with the material we have just explored.

When Thomas was a little child he lived in the Kingdom of his Father's House, and like Buddha, delighted in the wealth and splendor provided by his Father. Alas, this was not to last. His Parents sent him out from his Homeland on an arduous spy mission, with provisions for the journey...

From the wealth of their treasuries they gave him a great but light cargo (or "burden" as in Matthew 11:30, "My yoke is easy but my burden is light"). The cargo, we are told in *HOP*, was *gold* from the *high country* ("the above").

They lifted or removed from pure Thomas the "jewel-studded garment shot with gold" ( ) -- the Robe of Glory or Cloak of Light (the Illumined Ones, the Illuminati) -- which in their love, says *HOP*, they had made for him. This 'robe of yellow' (*golden?*) was tailored to his size ("age").

Thomas's parents made a covenant (arch) with him, and wrote it in his mind so that he would not forget it.

And they said to Thomas, when he goes down into Egypt and brings up the One Pearl which lies in the middle of the sea, and which is encircled by the fiery and ravenous (or "swallowing") dragon, he will put back on that jewel-studded Cloak of Glory, and will become the herald (or Oracle) for his parent's Kingdom, along with his twin brother (Jesus).

So Thomas left the East, and accompanied by two guides, made his way into the land of the Babylonians. In the notes to the *HOP*, Layton observes that "Babylon" is not the Mesopotamian city on the Euphrates. Rather, it refers to the Egyptian "Babylon," a fortified city in the vicinity of the Great Pyramid.[5]

The Egyptian Osiris or Meru pillar links the Egyptian and Babylonian Babylons. The design of the Tower of Babel was based upon the Su-Meru pillar, which Mongolian myth says was an antenna-like pillar that produced a ring of life that kept the immortals immortal. Significantly, *tower* rings of *tour*, meaning a circle or circuit, and a ring , or Oracle. Babel was supposed to have had seven rings (corresponding with the seven notes and the seven heavens). It may be equated with the Gaelic *tor*, meaning a conical hill or a castle called a *nob* or *neb*, meaning a crossing point. A drawing found at the

temple of Anu, E.A.'s father, at Uruk depicts the "mighty APIN ("an object that plows through" or *opens*, but which resembles the *nib* of a *pin* or a *pen*), perhaps a model for the Tower of Babel. Without the vowels, APIN is

PN, the same as the Gnostic beam or particle of the spiritual substance of the Oracle, Epinoia. This is the subject of Thomas's quest.

The three wise men, Thomas and his two guides, went straight to the dragon and settled down close by his inn until the dragon should sleep, so that he could take the Pearl from him. Thomas wore a disguise so that the locals would not suspect him of coming from Abroad to steal the Pearl. But the locals ingratiated themselves to him, and mixed him a drink with their cunning, so that he forgot that he was a King's son, and served their king. And he forgot the Pearl for which his parents had sent him.

Watching their son from above, Thomas's parents convene the royal court. It is decided that he should not be left in Egypt. And they write Thomas a letter saying, "From thy Father, the King of kings, greetings.... Awake and arise out of thy sleep, and listen to the words of our letter. Remember that you are a King's son. You have fallen under a servile yoke (⌣⌢⌣). Remember your garment shot with gold. Remember the Pearl for which you were sent on the mission to Egypt.

Thomas's parents were additionally concerned about the demons of the Labyrinth, a famous and extremely intricate temple complex southwest of modern Cairo near Crocodilopolis, home of the Crocodile god Sobek. The Greek version of the *HOP*, says Layton, implies that the Pearl and its guardian "dragon" are in the Labyrinth.[6]

Herodotus regarded the Labyrinth as far more incredible than the pyramids themselves, and as an eye witness, minutely described it.

Herodotus says that he found therein 3,000 chambers; half subterranean and the other half above ground. He examined the upper chambers in detail. Into the underground ones, the keepers of the building would not let him go, for they contained the sepulchers of the kings who built the Labyrinth, and also those of the sacred crocodiles. He found the upper passages were filled with exquisitely carved figures. At the corner of the Labyrinth stands a pyramid forty fathoms high, with large figures engraved upon it, and it is entered by a vast subterranean passage.

Thomas listened to the voice (the Oracle) of the letter from his parents. And, says *HOP*, what was written in the letter was also engraved upon his heart. And on that spot or dot (no doubt an oracle or place of communication with the deity), he remembered that he was a child of kings a 'noble one' ('Ayran', 'Mighty One', 'Christ').

He also remembered the Pearl for which he had been sent on this spy mission and that he had to steal or 'lift' it from the Dragon or Serpent.

Thomas subdued the Dragon by calling his Father's name (A Tone, in the Language of the Birds). He lifted the Pearl, released himself from his earthly skin and began to make his way to the road leading home to his parents. Along the way, a female being (the ray of the Oracle Epinoia?) lifts him up. "So she got me up from sleep," wrote Thomas, "giving as it were an *oracle* by (her) voice, with which *she guided me to the light*".

Buzzing with a feeling of familial love (AMOR) leading and drawing him on, Thomas passed by the Labyrinth, left Babylon and entered the *Meson* or intermediate realm.

Upon arriving Thomas could not recall his jewel stud suit. But then, suddenly, in a "mirror, mirror on the wall moment", he saw his garment reflected as in a mirror. He perceived it in his whole self as well *and through it gained acquaintance* with it he learned that he was made of the same material as the image in the mirror. Upon recognizing this he is given his *garment of bright colors* (a coat of many colors or Cloak of Light) as his reward. This garment was "embroidered with gold, precious stones, and pearls to give a suitable impression. It was clasped at the collar, and the image of the King of Kings was (woven) all through it; Stones of lapis lazuli had been agreeably fixed to the collar. And he saw, in turn, that *impulses* or *motions* of *Gnosis* were rippling through it called *ef-ful-gence.*

The talking, blue stone encrusted Cloak spoke to Thomas. "It is I who belong to the one who is stronger than all human beings and for whose sake I was designed by the father himself…"

Thomas reached out, took the cloak and put it on his body.

Once he put it on he arose into the realm of Peace (Tula).

THE BLUE PEARL

Thomas was the name of the disciple who was sent to India. In the East the Pearl that Thomas snatched from the dragon and that made him an Oracle is called the Blue Pearl and is considered a physical manifestation of the soul. It is called the Seed of Buddha Nature.[7] The pearl being spherical ◯ is regarded as a symbol of the Soul or Spirit lying encased within the human body.

It is the actual form of the Self, our innermost reality, the form of God, which lives within us. Everyone can see, feel or experience the Blue Pearl.

When kundalini energy (the God Force that ascends our inner Tree of Life) becomes active through mantra meditation and rises through the seven chakras many see a subtle blue dot appear and disappear on their mental screen during meditation. The blue dot is referred to as the Blue Pearl by Swami Muktananda and is referred to as the most significant of meditation experiences.[8] The scriptures describe this Blue Pearl as the divine light of Consciousness, which dwells within everyone.

When the Blue Pearl expands, writes Swami Muktananda in *Secret of the Siddhas*, an extraordinary Blue Being manifests from the center of its center.[9] This being is called the Blue Lord (*Epinoia?*). A visualization of the Blue Being is considered to be the realization of the form of God.

I call this Blue Being the Oracle, the part that connects or patches us in to the God Head.

From our examination of the Gnostic texts we know the "Oracle" is within the divine core of every human. It is the job of the Oracle to awaken our awareness of the "immortal core" and our Divine Particle with its spiritual potential imprinted within. The Oracle is the (blue) *god* within that *guides* the Fool within us into the *guild* of the Craft (the Ship); *guld*, *gold* or *god making*. This part of ourselves is "lost at sea" and must be "found".

The Blue Pearl.

The Blue Dragon is the guardian of the Blue Apple,
Stone or Pearl.

*'The Man in Sapphire Blue" by Hildegard of Bingen.
Jesus, the Blue Being.*

The Egyptians conceived KNEPH, *the father of Ptah, as a blue being. His name,* KNEPH, *is the root of Knephis, Chnoupis, or Chnoubis.* CANOPIS means 'ship'.

The Blue Being, the embodiment of God Consciousness, is made of an extraordinary light, says Swami Muktananda.[10] Just as Consciousness expands (or pulsates), pervades the entire universe, and once again contracts, similarly the Blue Being, Consciousness, the Great Light once again becomes the Blue Pearl, as tiny as a sesame or mustard seed, and re-enters the body *through the eyes.*

The visualization of the Blue Being leads to complete knowledge. This *effulgence fills* the initiate (the *fool*) *full* of *gen*, the Mayan word for Love.

The Blue Being can be found at the center of all the world's great esoteric traditions. The Hindu Lord Krishna (or Kristna) is blue. Vishnu (or Fish-Nu), because of his association with water, is depicted blue; therefore all his incarnations including Krishna, are shown as such. Sky is the reflection of Krishna's bodily effulgence; therefore it is blue. In Hinduism, persons who have depth of character and the capacity to fight evil are depicted as blue skinned. The blue skinned people are considered a lost race.

In *One Hundred Thousand Years of Man's Unknown History* French author Robert Charreaux suggests that the inhabitants of Atlantis were blue skinned people. When they resettled after the cataclysm of Atlantis their skin tone paled.

Today, the hills and hollows of eastern Kentucky ring with tales of the "blue people" who enjoy vibrant health well into old age.[11]

The Ainu, an indigenous people living in Japan whose skin hue is often described as blue tell of being who came from space and created the Ainu. I find it most interesting that the *Ainu* legend so closely matches the Sumerian chronicles of the *Annu-naki*.

According to master symbolist Harold Bayley, the Norse savior *Odin* is said to have worn a *blue* coat, a connection to the Blue Being and the Cloak of Light. Druidic High Priests, like the Jewish Head Priest, wore *blue* robes. Plato said the Head Priests of Atlantis wore "the most beautiful azure robes."[12] Mary also wore a *blue* robe. She was 'sky clad'.

Bayley notes that the Celts and Maoris tattooed themselves in *blue* paint. The blue paint used for this purpose was called *Woad*, which probably came from *Wodan, Wodan* or *Odin*. Woad is also a pun on *the Wood* or *the Word*. *Odin* is easily exchanged with *Otin*, O-Atin or ATON.

The expression *blue blooded*, and the meaning of the blue skin, I believe, originally symbolized the idea of having the wisdom of the Word, the Divine Blue Being, pulsing in one's veins (*vines*). The closer one was to becoming the Blue Being the bluer one's blood ran and the bluer one's skin became.

Bayley notes that the Greek for *blue* – bel Hue, beautiful hue – is *glaukos* (*gleaming, blue-ish green, silvery*).[13] *Glaucodot* ('blue dot') is a graying, tin-white mineral composed of arsenic, cobalt, iron and sulphur. It is hard to see since it reflects all light. Glaucodot comes from the Greek for "blue," in reference to its use in the dark blue glass called smalt. Smalt is ground glass of blue color and was the earliest of the cobalt blue pigments. Its origin is not clear.

The French for blue is *vrai*, similar to the Italian *vero* or *excellente*. Vrai and Vero ring of *virile* and *vril*, the secret of the Aryans sought by the Nazis that, in my system, transmuted ordinary human blood into the blood of the Aryan (*Ari* or Lion People). The *Ari*, "the first," are akin to the *Illi*, the Light (blue?) Ones.[14] The word *heir* or *hari* leads to the belief that the Ari are the children of the Illi ('light') gods. The oracle is literally the word of the 'le' or Illi spoken from behind the veil of skin. Names such as Mari, Hiram, as well as Cath-ari, are variations of the word Ari. All are part human, part Illi.

Ari-ael is what the perfect called Yaldabaoth.[15] Ari-ael can mean *ari* 'true', 'blue' *el* 'light'.

Akhenaton as the Sphinx. Ariael is what the perfect call Yaldabaoth because he was like a lion (Ari in Hebrew). In the hierarchy of angels Ariael is the Lion of God.

Can you imagine a seed essence within yourself, a Divine Blue Particle -- also called a Blue Apple, a Blue Stone or a Blue Pearl – that blossoms into a new (blue) skin or garment and opens gateways in space that allow instant access to galaxies billions of miles away… paths that take us back to the Source (Pleroma)?

The pearl brings important illumination and guidance as an alchemical metaphor for this study. For alchemists the Blue Stone is not an external jewel. This pearl is inside the human body and may be the new (*gnu* or *knu*) substance called *brain sand* that modern scientists have discovered localized in the pineal gland – the third eye gland that secretes Serotonin, Melatonin, DMT, 5-meo-DMT and Pinoline, the last three of which are psychoactive. During the multiple cycles or stages of illumination of the Oracle, this sand gradually becomes purified, refined and eventually fuses into a single body (more later). Unlike other gems oysters, a living organism, produce pearls as the result of an injury. It usually begins forming around a grain of sand or an egg of some parasite that invaded the oyster. The oyster protects itself by layering the irritant with nacre -- mother-of-pearl -- until, out of pain and suffering, it forms an object of great beauty. The offending particle actually becomes a gem of great worth.

So it is with us spiritually. "There was a time," says Plato, "when we were not yet sunk into this 'tomb', which now we bear about with us and call it 'body', bound fast (to

it) like an oyster ∞ (to its shell) .[16] According to the

Gnostics, we are the products of a botched creation, an injury inflicted by Sophia.

We can make a second comparison with our bodies. The pearl is first embedded in a mass of live but corruptible flesh, then separated and cleansed from its surroundings so that it can appear in its purity and beauty. So it is with our Cloak of Light or light body. It is deeply cloaked in a mystery and must be unveiled before it can return home. As long as the pearl (the light body) remains cloaked in the oyster (the flesh) it is of no value.

The production of the pearl is a gradual, even tedious, process. Slowly, the oyster adds layer after thin layer of nacre until the iridescent pearl is transformed. So it is with the human body. As mentioned in the introduction, since the 13th century a movement has been afoot to add a new layer of technology (a 'new iridescent skin') to the body to manifest personal miracles and to free us from our flaws or injuries.

Drawing the comparisons further, we know the ah-oyster is a ship at home in the depths of the ocean, a scavenger living off the garbage that sinks to the bottom of the sea. Revelation 13:1 shows the beast (the Pearl) rising out of a sea: "Then I stood on the sand of the sea. And I saw a beast rising up out of the sea, having seven heads and ten horns, and on his horns ten crowns, and on his heads a blasphemous name."

The Beast is the grain of sand that becomes a (blue) Pearl. The Sea is the Sea of Glass, the cosmic aquarium created by Yaldabaoth and described as the Throne of Christ in Revelation. The seven heads that enable us to grow our horns (rays) are the seven-fold sciences.

We are challenged to remove the pearl within us from the Sea of Glass, just as the oyster must be lifted from the mush of the sea bottom.

After the awakening of the Blue Pearl or Stone one is 'Type II Illuminati', i.e. capable of building a bridge (or Ark) of blue light between Heaven and Earth, matter and mind. Like Jung, John Rossner, Ph. D. has claimed awakening the Pearl included a "divine alchemy," the goal of which was self-transformation and the transformation of humanity towards a divine state of being and to "become for a time as mighty as the original possessor of the power."[17] The "apotheosized" or "divinized" human heroes, the Oracles, were described as "new beings".[18]

As described by Sir E.A. Wallis Budge, here's a list of earthly feats the Oracle is capable of performing:

○ Healing the sick.

○ Returning the dead to life.

○ "Clothing" or "cloaking" his followers in an "incorruptible body," a light body, as did Jesus.

○ Weather control.

○ Manipulation of matter.

○ Predicting the future.

○ Altering the past (and future).[19]

From my initial analysis of the myths of these Blue Stones, presented in my books *Blue Apples* and *Cloak of the Illuminati*, I have hypothesized that the Blue Stones are an exotic matter that the gods used to create gateways ◯ and pass through to other realms. Today, we call exotic matter *monoatomic elements*. The ancients called it *manna*. The works of Laurence Gardner have made it amazingly clear that modern science has rediscovered the ancient science manna as an exotic matter that can open holes in space through which, one day, humans will be able to pass through to other realms.[20] I find it remarkably intriguing to compare the ancient gateway stories to the modern theories of stargates and wormholes.

For instance, the Book of Numbers (13), another "spy story", tells us Joshua, son of Nun (= Fish) stole these Blue Stones, symbolized by a cluster of enormously heavy grapes, from E.A.'s tribe of gods, the Anunnaki ('those who came from heaven'), at the valley of Eschol and returned them to Moses along with a warning, "the land there eateth the people up". I have interpreted this cryptic phrase as meaning the gods were operating a gateway, an Oracle center that caused people to vanish through a ◯ of light, similar to the orb in which the Terminator time travels in the movie *Terminator 3*. The Blue Stones or "*Blue Apples*," as they are also known, symbolized this gateway and the secret of the Oracle.

Autumn, Grapes of the Promised Land, by Nicholas Poussin. Joshua and Caleb steal the cluster of grapes, the Blue Stones, from the gods at Eschol.

Joshua and Caleb deliver the Blue Stones or Apples, ⚥ *,*
to the Crucifixion. The Tree of Life or Cross of Crucifixion
of Jesus is the vine of the Grape.

The Bible is mute concerning what Moses did with the Blue Stones of the gods. This is strange considering they possibly represent the core secrets of the universe. In fact, the cluster of grapes became a cryptogram for the Church itself.

These Blue Stones are believed to be sapphire crystals containing cosmic secrets 'etched by the hand of God'. Talmudic-Mishraic sources say they were transparent, flexible, blue and like the grapes of Eschol were very heavy. Later, I will connect these Blue Stones with the Urim and Thummim stones worn on the breastplate of Moses's brother, Aaron, the Hebrew Oracle. It is the jewel greatly coveted by kings.

Graham Hancock mentions these 'stones' in *The Sign and the Seal*, speculating that Moses knew they were hidden on Mount Sinai and that they are meteorites possessing a supernatural power source.[21] Further, he suggests they are a cipher for the Holy Grail.

The word sapphire used to describe these stones may be a mistranslation of *sappur*, 'holy blood', says Robert Graves.[22] Ezekiel mentions it as the color of the Throne of God.[23] True Blue.

As portrayed in the depiction of Joshua and Caleb delivering the grapes stolen from the Promised Land to the Crucifixion from the Castle of Valere in Sion, Switzerland, on the previous page, Gnostic Christian tradition maintains the Blue Stones (or their secrets) were present at the Gul-Gotha, the place of the Skull or Head, where Jesus crafted the Holy Blood and the Holy Water within his body during the Crucifixion. Interestingly, *Gul* or *Gal* is Keltic for *stone*, *column* or *pillar*.[23]

111

The allusion to the head and the vine (*vein*) draws us to the early Hebrew belief that the vine (the ladder, the stairway to heaven, the DNA coils) was humankind's greatest possession.[25] It possessed and insured life and made life worth living. Mark (12:6) says that God was the man who planted the vine and who asked his son to visit his vineyard. The followers of John the Baptist, the *Mandaeans*, used the word 'vine' not only to denote the Heaven-sent One, but also a whole series of beings from the upper world of light.[26]

This may even include *Epinoia*. Following the horse pun enfolded in her name we find a correlation between the words *wine* and *winne* or *whine* the sound made by nag or horse.

THE PEARL OF GREAT PRICE

The forgoing prepares us to interpret one of the greatest parables of Jesus the Pearl of Great Price, which serves as a parable of the kingdom of God. This parable is unique to the Gospel of Matthew, although a version of the story occurs in the Gnostic *Gospel of Thomas*. The Pearl of Great Price predates Matthew; it was perhaps an original composition by Jesus.

"Again, the kingdom of heaven is like unto a merchant man, seeking goodly pearls: Who, when he had found one pearl of great price, went and sold all that he had, and bought it." [27]

"Again, the kingdom of heaven is like unto a treasure hid in a field; the which when a man hath found, he hideth, and for joy thereof goeth and selleth all that he hath, and buyeth that field."[28]

The Pearl of Great Price is often presented as a twin to The Treasure in the Field of Matthew 13:44 inasmuch as both relate the kingdom (*Plane?*) of God (also described as a *Sea of* Glass, a *Net* or the *Matrix*) to a discovered treasure; however, the emphasis of the two differs. Whereas the parable of the Treasure in the Field focuses on the joyous surprise of finding the kingdom, the parable of the Pearl of Great Price discusses a situation in which the kingdom is purposefully sought by a merchant. In this parable the merchant "anticipates the element of surprise" in that he intently seeks out the pearl and the value held therein.

The word "merchant" has had an interesting evolution. It originally meant a passenger on a ship, a merchant marine, but gradually became applied to the wholesale dealer as distinguished from a retailer.

In the Nag Hammadi text, *The Acts of Peter and the Twelve Apostles*, the traveling apostles sail to a land where they meet a cloaked physician who reveals himself to be Jesus.[29] Jesus gives the apostles an unguent (*anointing*) box and a pouch full of medicine with instructions to go heal. Prior to giving them the pouch, Jesus announces to all in the streets, "Pearls! Pearls!" Seeing no evidence that Jesus actually possesses pearls (in the physical sense) the wealthy pass him by. The poor, however, who are eager for a first hand look at a real pearl, hang around. He tells them, "If it

113

is possible, come to my city, so that I may not only show it before your eyes, but give it to you for nothing."

These sacred tones of the Pearl Merchant are used to allow us to shift through the veil of creation and sail (like Enki) into or *pass through to* ◯ the realm of pure unity of matter and energy. Traditional shamanic peoples around the world say the Blue Stone or Apple is actually how our soul travels to the inner realm and it is inside of a *quantum egg* or in an *"interphasic state of existence"* (able to jump through time and cross great distances or even to use this skill locally). Christian art portrays Jesus (or Thomas, his twin) riding in a ring of blue tones, illustrating awareness of these secrets.

Jesus rides on the Blue Stone. Ravenna, Italy.

Jesus (or Thomas?) rides in the Blue Stone.

The Blue Stone is portrayed as an orb, globe, egg, cloud, mist or even a *Hexagon* (Star of David) in three dimensions. This is also known as the Mer-Ka-Ba, the symbol of the Divine in us all that is activated by energy fields from the God Head . The 'alchemist' is the one who finds the 'philosopher's stone'. In some alchemical texts, this wisdom is illustrated as a Hexagon with a dot above the right point. It represents the presence of God. This dot is the Blue Apple.

In ancient Egypt, the blue water lily (flower of light) was brought by Nefertem, the god of perfume, and was also symbolic of rebirth after death.[30] Tutankhamen's innermost gold coffin had blue water lily petals scattered over it along with a few other floral tributes. Rumors of secret chambers in the Great Pyramid filled with fine blue dust abound.

The Egyptians looked forward to their souls coming to life "like a water lily reopening", thinking that the deceased died as the water lily closed awaiting opening with the morning sun. The *Book of the Dead* has a spell to allow the deceased to transform into one of these flowers:

In this drawing of the Egyptian **blue** *stone bowl, three fish gather at a point in a circle* ⊙*, the hieroglyph for sun, light, gold, the Milky Way's G-Spot and the Milky Way herself. It symbolizes the supreme spiritual principle. The lotus blossoms symbolize unfolding awareness.*

(The Chapter of) Making the Transformation into the Water Lily reads:

The Osiris Ani, whose word is truth, saith: "I am the holy water lily that cometh forth from the light *which belongeth to the nostrils of Ra*, and which belongeth to *the head of Hathor*. I have made my way, and I seek after him, that is to say, Horus. I am the pure blue water lily that cometh forth from the field (of Ra)."

The perfume of this flower was not only pleasing to the Egyptians, but they saw it as healing as well. Scenes show women holding the water lily and people being offered the flower ·at parties, smelling its divine fragrance. Some people today believe that the Egyptians used this plant as a narcotic both for its healing qualities and as a recreational drug when soaked in wine, though this is a hotly debated topic.

The Gnostics adopted the Egyptian blue lily symbolism. In the alchemical *Book of the Holy Trinity* from Germany we find a remarkable depiction of the cross of Jesus growing as a blue lily out of the Holy Virgin Mari who kneels on the crescent moon. The lily with the five petals, says Titus Burckhardt, corresponds to the *Quintessence*. Twelve stars, with Jesus as the twelfth, surround the egg of the Mother, who corresponds to Sophia and the *material prima*, the soul substance.

The cross of Christ growing as a blue lily out of Mary who kneels on a crescent moon. From a miniature in the alchemical Book of the Holy Trinity, *in the Staatsbibliothek, Munich.*

The lily with the five petals, like the five-petaled rose, corresponds to the *Quintessence*, and the Mother of God corresponds to the mother matter.

There are fascinating Buddhist parallels to Gnostic, Cathar and Rosicrucian symbolism. Buddha, the 'Great Enlightener' is often portrayed emerging from an open lotus, his head surrounded by a halo of light. The lotus was originally the flower of Lilith who is also Is-Tara or Astarte, the Sumero-Babylonian Goddess of creation.[31] The northern Europeans called her *Eostre*, the Goddess of "Easter" lilies.[32] In medieval times the Easter lily was the pas-flower or Paschal flower, from the Latin *passus*, to step or *pass over*, cognate of *pascha*, the Passover.[33] The pagans believed that when Hera's milk spurted from her breasts to form the Milky Way, the drops that fell to the ground became lilies.[34] These drops of matter from the Galactic G-Spot were the "blue stones" or "blue apples" that transformed men into Shining Ones or gods able to *pass*

through (Yaldabaoth) $\bigcirc$ to the realm of light. When Jesus was depicted as a blue lily, I believe it signified his transformation into a Shining One, Illumined One or an Illuminati.

6.

THE REALM OF THE ILLUMINATI

From the forgoing we have learned that, in the Gnostic view, the soul is a ship a bottle ⬬ or a divine pearl in an oyster. Human beings are merchant ships in a strange port. Though imprisoned in the evil "matter" of earth, humanity carries within itself the leftover *sparks* of the precosmic **Pleroma** that existed before the creation of humanity. These sparks are called the Blue Pearl.

Our body *cloaks* this spiritual "spark". We must be decloaked for us to rediscover our true being and to return to the primordial state of the Pleroma where, says Jung, there is a perfect interplay of cosmic forces. [1]

The Gnostics (including the Cathars) sought to be "aware of the pleroma" in a profound way -- to feel the fullness of it within their (foolish) selves. Jung comments that the Pleroma is "a state of *fullness* where the pairs of opposites, yea and nay, day and night, are together..." This matches comments such as this, from the *Gospel of Thomas*:

Jesus said to them, "When you make the two one, and when you make the inside like the outside and the outside like the inside, and the above like the below, and when you make the male and the female one and the same, so that the male not be male nor the female; ...then will you enter the kingdom"

The Pleroma is the evolutionary leap beyond human in the writings of Dane Rudhyar, author of *The Astrological Mandala.*

It is a planetary Communion with the Higher Source, the God Head.

It transcends all cultures.

Interestingly, in the Greek lexicon the pleroma is a word for a *ship filled* with sailors.

"What we call mankind," observes Rudhyar, "is but the long, gradual, arduous, often tragic, and always dangerous transition between the level of 'life' — as we know it in the earth's biosphere, where it operates as a quasi-instinctual and compulsive type of homogeneity — and that of the Pleroma."

The highest possibility of consciousness operates in this Pleroma state. It is here we find the ultimate human, (the Oracle). "Subconsciously, if not consciously," says Rudhyar, "humanity aspires to such a state because it is humanity's function on this planet to be the transition between two levels of being: the vegetable and Pleroma states."[3]

ENKI'S SCHOOL FOR THE BLIND

According to the Gnostics, during the travails described in *Hypostasis of the Archons*, *The Apocryphon of John* and

The Hymn of the Pearl the "true" (*blue*) God, observing these events from the *Pleroma*, decides to help humankind, who, though unknowingly and helplessly trapped in evil and corrupt matter, nonetheless contains a spark of divinity (the Blue Stone, Pearl or Apple), which longs to rejoin the

God Head   , if only it could escape the body and the Earth.

Thus, the highest God sends the serpent to the garden to help Adam and Eve in their plight. This serpent is not a lowly reptile. In the original Sumerian telling of this tale, the serpent is E.A. or Enki the god of smith craft, technology and alchemy who, we are told, came to Earth on a rescue mission after the destruction of the *Maiden of Life* or *Watery Dragon of Chaos*, Tiamat, in search of gold and blue stones that cause illumination. He is said to have manufactured the human body as a slave vehicle in order to mine gold. His half brother, Enlil, opposed him.

E.A.'s story bears a powerful resemblance to Yaldabaoth or Ia-du baoth's. *Ia El Da* or *Ia El Du* is evidently the Shining Deus or the 'divine god' *Ia* or *Ie*. This is Ia or E.A., whose temple-medical facility was called *Eri-Du* or Ari-Du. It was at *Eri-Du*, an ancient religious center in Iraq (ancient Su-Meru), that Enki and his assistants created the human body.[4] These assistants, called *malachim*,[5] (who match the description of the archons of Yaldabaoth) are pictured on page 125.

Like the Hebrew god Jehovah, Yaldabaoth may be a composite of both Enki and Enlil, the twin principles in conflict with one another. Enki seeks to uplift humanity, even to the level of the gods. Enlil seeks to oppress humanity and squelch its potential. The story of Enki is told from the Enlilian perspective (as the Gnostic Christian story is told from the orthodox Church's view). From this view Enki appears as the troublemaking serpent whose wisdom is to be avoided.

From the Gnostic or alchemical perspective, when we are told Enki came to Earth to mine gold it points to his true purpose: to mine or 'save' souls. I have proposed elsewhere that he came to Earth to rescue the souls of Tiamat, an exploded planet described as a watery dragon of Chaos, and whose story is strikingly reminiscent of Sophia and Yaldabaoth's.

E.A. toasts a man emerging from a receptacle.

*The 'malachim' or assistants of Enki? From the
Baghdad Museum.*

In the Gnostic way, the human body, as a container of life force spun from DNA, is a receptacle *and* a flow-er, in particular, of souls. It is a mechanical contraption that is to be used for the soul to return to the Pleroma.

It was at Eridu that Enki taught the secrets of the ME Tablets or (S)tones of Destiny. After Enki gave him the ME, Adapa, the first man, was nicknamed NUN.ME, or "He who can decipher the MEs" Stones of Light (Stones of the Oracle). For thousands of years the saying "Wise as Adapa" conveyed the idea that someone was exceptionally wise, an Oracle. An early Sumerian ruler invited by the gods to ascend to the heavens was named EN.ME.DUR.AN.KI, which literally meant "ruler whose *ME* connect Heaven and Earth" or "Master of the Divine Tablets Concerning the Heavens."

NUN (*None, zero*) means "fish" in Hebrew. In Sumer physician-priests wearing fish cloaks identified themselves as emissaries of Enki. This class of priest-healers was known as *ashipu* or a-**ship**-u, exorcist priests who were masters of the spells that could drive away sickness. In the Assyrian depiction on the next page they are seen functioning as oracles.

The fish symbolism links with the Hindu Blue Being Vishnu or Fishnu and the early Christians who called themselves "sons of the celestial Fish or the Great Fish". "We small fish," wrote Tertullian in the second century, "like our Fish, Jesus Christ, swim in the (baptismal) water, and we can be saved only by remaining in it." And in the following century, St. Cyprian expressed the same belief: "It is in the water that we are reborn, in the likeness of Christ, our Master, the Fish."

126

Priests of the fish god E.A. tend a radiant **i** *pillar surmounted by a winged ring* ◯ *ridden by E.A.   Mer means sea, but also love. The* **mer-man** *are the priests of love.*

Compare the two fish and pillar above with fish and pillar in this early Christian symbol from the catacombs in Rome.

127

The early Christian symbol of the *anchor* with fish grasping a line of hope is plainly kin to, if not a copy of, the Sumerian seal portraying the fish priests beside the radiant Pillar above which hovers Enki, lord of Eridu.

Eridu is easily rendered E-Ray-Du, and *dew* is the same as *duv* (dove), the symbol of Sophia, the *Holy Spirit*. The Hebrew word *a-dow*, to wash, is the same as *dew* (vowels are interchangeable). The Egyptian hieroglyph *mst* (mist) resembles a three-fold fall of radiating water (Enki was the Lord of Water) or *rays* , and the pawnbroker's (merchant's) symbol . It means "celestial tears" or "*dew*,"[6] and portrays *three* drops of water (*stars*) falling or radiating from Heaven. The same hieroglyphic also means "instruction" or "teaching."[7]

Harold Bayley notes that the three circles in this Cathar symbol are called *Perfect Love*, *Perfect Wisdom* and *Perfect Power*.[8] These came from the sacrifice of the 'head' of the serpent, says Bayley. In my opion, the 'head' in question is the Oracle's Stimulator of the Cosmic G-Spot, the , which features the levitating serpent (or tone) and a head or pillar symbol that, once again, matches

128

the Cathar symbols and . Bayley connects the sacrifice of the head – the spiritual essence produced by this device -- to the Mayan symbolism of the Great Serpent of Power *Canah*. As I have noted, Joshua went into *Cannan* – Canah, the Serpent – to retrieve the Blue Apples.

In the Cathar emblems shown here the letter A forms the foundation of a flame-like tree, spinal column or Fire of Life. This rod or stem of Jesse (Jesus), says Bayley,[9] may be equated with the Ashera or Is-*Tara* Pillar, which answers to the Pillar of Osiris.

These three rays correspond with the three rays entering the forehead of the pupal Osiris shown previously. Intriguingly, they are also the three 'rays' or beams of light of the letter 'A'. This symbol takes us to the heart of the Oracle mysteries. As we will see in the next chapter, the 'A' connects Oracles through time, including Sir Francis Bacon, the great scholar of Elizabethean England.

Secret societies were common in the Middle Ages, and Bacon, claims Mrs. Henry Potts in *Francis Bacon and His Secret Society*, was the center of a secret league for the advancement of learning. This revival of learning was the "New Birth of Time" – the "Renaissance.

Bacon's most intimate friends, relations and correspondents the Rosicrucians, the Illuminati and the Freemasons speak in their books of the necessity for a "universal language," notes Potts. This language is two-fold, partly signs, but mostly symbols or emblems. It is the language of the "Renaissance." The greatest flowering of this language is in the works of Francis Bacon.

Much mystery surrounds the life of Francis Bacon. About him it has been remarked that if there were a beam of knowledge derived from God upon any man, it was upon him. In the next chapter we will examine Bacon's connection to the Gnostic mysteries.

7.

FRANCIS BACON: ORACLE

That the letter A had some vital mysterious Gnostic
significance is evident from the words of Jesus found in the
The Gospel of the Infancy.[1] This apocryphal book tells us
that upon his return to Palla-Stone (Palestine) from Egypt
at approximately age 12 Jesus carved twelve clay birds and
turned them into live birds by rhythmically clapping his
hands over them. He was then sent to school to learn his
letters from Zaccheus, a Hebrew priest. Zaccheus wrote out
an alphabet for Jesus. He asked him to say Aleph, and
when he said aleph, Zaccheus made him say Beth. But
Jesus refused.

"And he looked upon the teacher Zacchaeus, and said
to him: Thou art ignorant of the nature of the Alpha, how
canst thou teach others the Beta? Thou hypocrite! First, if
thou knowest, teach the A, and we shall believe thee about
the B. Then he began to question the teacher about the first
letter, and he was not able to answer him. And in the
hearing of many, the child says to Zacchaeus: Hear, O
Teacher, the order of the first letter, and notice here how it
has lines, and a middle stroke crossing those which thou
seest common; (lines) brought together; the highest part
supporting them; and again bringing them *under one head*;

with three points (of intersection, ⋔); of the same kind;

131

principal and subordinate; of equal length. Thou hast the lines of the A. And when the teacher Zacchaeus heard the child speaking such and so great allegories of the first letter, he was at a great loss about such a narrative, and about his teaching."

At the end of this amazing discourse, Zaccheus was so surprised that he said, "*I believe this boy was born before Noah.*" He turned to Jesus' father, Joseph, and said, "thou has brought a boy to me to be taught, who is more learned than any master." He then turned to Mary and said, "*your son has no need of any learning.*"

This exchange clearly shows that the Hebrew priest believed Jesus was demonstrating his proficiency in pre-Flood (Atlantean?) knowledge concerning the alphabet.

We should not be surprised to find that the Cathars featured the mysteries of the letter A in their symbol system. The Cathar cross, on page 25, in which the letter 'A' emerges from the mouth of an ox that supports the cross, is evidence of this. As in the drawing shown here, the Cathar symbolists put two A's together ⋀⋀ to form the twin-peaked M, *the holy mountain*, with the cross in between. In this way the A and the M are joined.

The Essenes were highly influenced by the Babylonian god *Shem* or *Shamash* ('heavenly'), seen stepping through the gate with his Rod of Jesse in these depictions.

Shamash rises through the Egyptian ⊔ *or M.*

The sun god Shamash enters Earth through a gateway shaped like the Egyptian ⊔ *with a branch, wand or ray of light in his hand. Note that two cherubim guard the gate as in the later gate of Eden story.*

133

The M, we noted, symbolized the Oracle's Pillar/Stimulator that housed the rope of life , symbolic of the wormhole or stargate. This rope or tube can easily be twisted into the lower case 'a', or even the fish or 'life-line' symbol of Jesus .

The and the match the primary hieroglyph for the Egyptian bird of light, the heron , which is the symbol for the cosmic knot or bond, and predates Jesus by millennia. In Egyptian legend the heron delivered the key of life, a teaching designed to transform us into beings of light that, I believe, was taught in the Language of the Birds.

The priests who operated this Oracle are the 'birds of light'. They gave birth to an *oral* tradition maintained by the *bards* (poets) or *budd-has* (the awakened ones). These 'wise birds' transmitted the core knowledge of the 'oracular head' through the language of poetry and symbols. The light and **dark** A's are their signature. Bayley presumes this is an allusion to the idea expressed in the Vedas: "One of them shines brightly, the other is black; twin sisters are they, the one black, the other white."[2] They are the twin peaks.

In Sumerian myth, one of the gods of the As, , is Enlil, the other is Enki, who is also known as E.A., pronounced *A-ya*. The Greeks called these twins *anakes*, the One Great Light.

The Greatest Bard of all, William Shakespeare, is intimately connected with the A A symbolism. The Sonnets. Hamlet. King Richard. All bear the A A on their title pages.

*Two A's(mountains), one light and one **dark**, tail into*  *spirals* .

The A A also appears on the title page of the King James Bible (1611), which, it is claimed with great controversy, Sir Francis Bacon guided to fruition. The name Shake-Spear is a reference to Pallas-Athena, the Spear Shaker. When the King James Bible was published in 1611, Shakespeare was 46 years of age. The 46th word of Psalm 46 is "shake", and the 46th word from the end of

Psalm 46 is "spear"! The 46th Psalm connection looks impressive, but is pure coincidence, say critics, who maintain there is no real evidence that Shakespeare collaborated in translating the King James Bible. William Henry Smith, whose *Bacon and Shapespeare* was published in 1856, launched the Bacon is Shakespeare theory. In so doing he gave rise to a very powerful corpus of literature that links Shakespeare to Bacon. I'd like now to link Bacon, via the A **A**, to the Gnostic mysteries we have been discussing.

Bacon published books written by other authors under his direction. He had his own wood blocks of devices, some of which were his own design, and every book produced under his direction, whether written by him or not, was marked by the use of one or more of these wood blocks. These authors include Edmund Spenser, Christopher Marlowe, Shakespeare, Walter Raleigh, and others.[3] The favorite device was the light A and the dark **A**. Where did Bacon get this idea?

The following is from Mather Walker on the subject.[4]

While Francis Bacon was in France during the period from 1576 through 1579 a number of works were published exhibiting his A **A** handiwork. The A **A** also appeared in Alciato's Emblems, 'the little book' of riddles by the Italian genius Andrae Alciato (1492-1520) first published in 1531. Classified as a collection of religious love emblems or symbols Alciat's emblems tell the story of the religion of love, the religion of AMOR of the Cathars. From this, we are to assume that Bacon's use of the A **A** indicated the Gnostic origin of his works.

Whether or not he is Shakespeare Bacon (*Beaon*) is considered an illumined mind gifted with prophetic vision, and a true initiate who hid his secrets in cryptograms buried in works bearing the A A.[5] His extraordinary life and works have been rigorously investigated for more than two centuries. His intellectual accomplishments are widely recognized, particularly in academic occult circles, where he is recognized as a link in a great chain of enlightened teachers. He is regarded, noted Manly P. Hall, not as just a man, but rather as the focal point between an invisible institution and a world, which was never able to distinguish between the messenger and the message, which he promulgated.[6] This secret society, most often referred to as *Illuminati*, having rediscovered the lost secret sacred science sought to preserve and conceal this knowledge through symbols transmitted to its members. Bacon encoded these symbols within his works. By means of a certain key or code readers of these works could find the sacred science whereby a human is raised to the level of the illumined ones. He who solves the mystery of Bacon-Shakespeare will find the key to the lost wisdom of the Illuminati. Hall notes that the key to the Bacon mystery is the Seven-Rayed God.[7]

In my opinion, this is Chnoubis, aka Yaldabaoth.

THE GNOSTIC SECRET OF THE TEMPLARS

While living in Europe, Francis Bacon was initiated into the mysteries of the Order of the Knights Templar and the true secret of Masonic Origin.[8] His connection with them may be traced through his father, Sir Nicholas Bacon, the descendant, according to S. Baring Gould, of Jacques de Molay, 'the last Templar' martyred by Philip of France for his faith, 1314.[9] As Bacon's choice of symbols suggests, he learned a very special secret, and one shared by the Templars. (Interestingly, the Globe Theater where Shakespeare's plays were performed was octagonal, like the Templar churches, which were also circular.)

According to one provocative theory noted by Kenneth Mackenzie in his late 19th century Masonic encyclopedia, the original Templar Commanders were initiates to a secret affiliation of primitive Gnostic Christians under the leadership of the Patriarch Theoclete who had made High de Payens (the founder of the Templars) heir to the Apostolic Succession of John the Divine.[10] In other words, the founder of the Templar received a transmission from the Oracle.

Intriguingly, this Order is said to have transmitted a secret body of knowledge that passed along a succession through Jesus through Moses (whom many believe to have been Akhenaton). This figure was trained in all the Gnostic wisdom of the Egyptian magi. He taught or transmitted this wisdom down through the Essene/Kanobi discipleship to Jesus, through the Mediatrix (feminine co-Creator) Mary. In time, Jesus transmitted this knowledge to his apostles and disciples.

M. Matter and Eliphas Levi were two convinced that the origin of the Johannite Church could be traced to the sect of ancient Christians known as the Mandaeans or Mandaean Sabians, the name of the followers of John the Baptist. "Sabian" is a word derived from the Aramaic-Mandic verb "Saba" which means "baptized" or "dyed", "immersed in water". "Mandaeans" is derived from "menda" which means in the Mandiac language "knowledge". Thus, "Mandaean Sabians" means those who are baptized and who know the religion *of* God This is opposed to the religion *about* God.

Among the peculiar symbols of this Order of the Mandai (also known as the Wise of John and Christians of John) was the figure of *a severed head*, a reminder of the martyrdom of their first teacher to some, but actually standing for something far more profound.

Among the long list of distortions collected by the Holy Inquisition against the Templar Order a reference to the veneration of a head, interpreted as that of the devil or of Mohamet, was chief among the accusations.[11] Nevertheless whether under torture or not many Templars alluded to the image or idol of their Grand Master by the head of an old bearded man, venerating the idol as though it were God himself. This head was called BAPHOMET, a word of unknown meaning. Dead Sea Scroll scholar Hugh Schonfield used a Hebrew code called the Atbash cipher which substitutes the first letter of the alphabet for the last and the second letter for the second last and so to Baphomet. He found that it generates the Greek word **Sophia** or 'wisdom' in English, and that the head was feminine.[12] Had the Templars acquired the wisdom of Sophia, as in Athena, Isis, Mary Magdalene? That is, had they acquired the Pillar of the Oracle, the Stimulator of the Cosmic G-Spot?

Of even more interest to us is the theory that Baphomet was a corruption of *Abufihamat*.[13] The meaning of the word is "Father of Understanding" or "Father of Wisdom." It is a term used to refer to a Sufi Master. In Arabic, father is taken to mean Source. If this is the case, this could imply God or the God Head. The Templars were quite likely to have come in contact with Sufism while in the Holy Land and many believe they absorbed some of their practices into the Templar rituals.

Other accusations said that the Templars believed that "the *head* could save them; it could make them rich; it could make the trees flower and the land germinate." It likely was kept in a round church. The Templars made their churches *round* because this was the shape of the head ◯ (and of Solomon's Temple).[14]

The *Chronicles of St. Denis* by Guillaume Paradin states that the head seemed to be of flesh, with dog hairs, and without gold or silver ornamentation, but from the neck region to over the shoulders it was completely strewn with gold and precious jewels. The head had a *bluish color* and spots. It had a beard of black and white hairs, similar to the beard worn by some Templars.

Saint Denis was the Christianized remake of the wine god Dionysus in Paris. Like Orphic shrines of Dionysus, the shrine of St. Denis featured an oracular head. It was claimed that, having been decapitated at Mont Martre (Mount of Martyrs), Denis then carried his own skull to his abbey.[15]

St. Denis is a key repository for Templar secrets, including those of the Ark of the Covenant, which the Templars are said to have recovered from the site of Solomon's Temple in Jerusalem in the early 1100s. The medallion from a window at the cathedral of St. Denis, the first Gothic cathedral, shown on the next page represents the Ark of the Covenant (or the Sea of Glass, Aquaria) carried on four wheels and resembling a triumphal chariot. Inside the Ark is seen *water*, the Rod of Aaron and the tablets of the Law or *Torah* ♏. *Water symbolizes the manna.* As I have written elsewhere, this is the complete *dead head*, the Oracular Pillar of Osiris, and represents the dead *true, blue* 'talking head' of the Templars.

Medallion from a window at St. Denis, Paris. The Pillar is attached to the Ark, and is surrounded by the Lion, Bull, Man and Eagle.

We note that the Ark (the R.C.) is surrounded by the Lion, Bull, Man and Eagle symbols of the four Power Tools. Earlier, I noted that Mary Magdalene knew the All. This was revealed to be the four Egyptian Power Tools:

Uas -- the tree branch, commonly called the 'Key of the Nile'. (Egyptians called the Milky Way the "Nile in the Sky".)[16] *TET or Djed* (center) -- the Pillar of Osiris, *Ankh* - - 'life', and *Nib* – 'All', 'Lord', 'Master'.[17]

Adding the Egyptian meaning of the Power Tools together with the symbolism in the medallion at St. Denis, I propose the Templars recovered the Pillar of Is-Tara and with it the secrets of the Oracle: the way to stimulate the G-Spot of the Milky Way and receive the Divine Particles spit there from.

One of the most incredible galleries of this symbolism is found at Abydos, Egypt's oldest Oracle. The in the blue stone-encrusted emblem of Abydos on the next page is the logo for these sciences. A related symbol,

, is the Egyptian hieroglyph for *shd* (sehedj, *shed*) '*shine*' and will be looked at later.[18] The serpent symbol has many layers of meaning. One of which is the shedding of skin. Jesus *shed* his blood at the Crucifixion as an atoning sacrifice.[19] *Strong's* says *shed* means *pouring out*, as in the pouring out of the Holy Spirit.[20]

In terms of our exploration, it means *purring* out of or vibrating out of.

142

The Blue Stone encrusted emblem (ab) *is mounted on a (dju)* sign, *meaning 'mountain', to form a monogrammatic rendering of the Egyptian place name Abju, "Abydos.*

When the emblem ⚒ (*ab*) is mounted on a (*dju*) ⌣ sign, meaning 'mountain', it forms a monogrammatic rendering of the Egyptian place name *Abju*, "Abydos." As we have noted, Abydos is the 'Place of the Buzz ∿ or Tone of God that, when heard in the head, brings enlightenment.

The Emblem of Abydos.

In the emblem of Abydos on the previous page two 'cherubs' hold the Pillar containing the 'head' of Osiris , the Oracle, which, we can more easily note here, (s)peeks, like Shamash, from between an **M**, the holy mountain, or the A **A.**

The holy 'head' of Osiris speaking from between the M

answers to this Cathar emblem of the *holy pillar* at the *holy mountain*. This is, I believe, the *Cathar emblem for head of the Oracle recovered by the Templars* from the Holy Mountain 'Moriah'.

From these connections, and his use of the A **A** symbol it is reasonable to propose that Bacon (Shakespeare) was a modern holder of this office, a Spear Shaker, and that he drank from the same wisdom stream as the Cathars. We may even go so far as to speculate that Bacon possessed the 'talking head' of god that spewed the sacred sciences of the

Oracle . It taught him the original language of light, the Language of the Birds, and provided him with wisdom

145

on a superhuman scale.

It is not unreasonable to further propose that Francis Bacon was the emobidment of Sophia. According to a Gnostic hymn attributed to Simon Magus, Sophia "passed from body to body."[21]

Vital knowledge concerning Bacon's connection to the paper-marks of the Cathars is found in Mrs. Henry Pott's *Francis Bacon and His Secret Society*. She comments that Bacon and his society, the Rosicrucians, expanded and diversified these paper-marks.

There are three paper-marks which Mrs. Pott found were especially associated with Francis Bacon and his brother Anthony. They are to be seen throughout the printed books ascribed to Francis. These marks are:

1. The bunch or cluster of grapes.
2. The pot, or jug.
3. The double candlesticks (towers or pillars).

Mrs. Pott notes that few of Bacon's letters, and none of his acknowledged books are without one of these marks. They are included because they point to him as their author or acknowledge the touch of his hand as a reviser or editor of the book.

The cluster of grapes, says Mrs. Pott, signified to Bacon and his society the *fruit of true* knowledge or *Gnosis,* which gathered in *clusters.* Bacon, says Mrs. Pott, worked the wine press, collecting his clusters, and storing up the grape's precious juice sot that in due season it may be poured upon other men's vessels.

The pot or vase contained the *heavenly liquor o f*

knowledge.

In Cathar paper-marks pots and jugs are shown spewing bunches of grapes – the fruits of knowledge – and *pearls* – the dew of heaven – or *manna*, the food of the gods.

The manna, we recall, was stored in the Ark of the Covenant along with the *golden pot* and *Aaron's rod that budded.* Here is, therefore, a connection between manna, a pot, the rod that, I believe, is attached to the Ark, and Sir Francis Bacon.

The manna was found by the Israelites in the early morning, after the dew evaporated, and before the *sun had risen* to melt it. *Manna, the dew* 𝍱 𝍰 or *rays* ⅍ and the *rise of the sun,* ⅊ , ⏀ .

The double candlesticks are the double A **A**s, the twin peaks through which the Son emerges.

ORACLE OF THE ILLUMINATI

8.

ABYDOS AND THE HEAD OF SOPHIA

In order to fully understand the Oracle we must briefly explore the Egyptian Temple of Seti at Abydos, the one time home of the head of Osiris and its stand.[1]

Abydos is Egypt's oldest royal cemetery. The ancient Egyptians said that at sunset, the area around this holy land looked like a golden staircase leading to the afterlife, and thus many people wished to be buried here. It's the location where, in myth, Osiris came back to power after being deceived by his brother, Seth, god of the moon.

The Temple of Seti is conveniently located beside the Osirion, an extremely ancient temple considered to be the tomb of Osiris. King Seti (1294-1279 BC), we are told by modern commentator Omm Sety, built the temple at Abydos to honor Osiris in accordance with the demands of a divine oracle.[2] She attributes the unusual L pattern of the Seti Temple to the unexpected rediscovery of the Osirion by Seti's craftsmen when constructing his temple.

Various commentators, including Omm Sety, argued that Seti had foreknowledge of the location of the Osiron (from the oracle) and located his temple there in order to discover and connect it to the Osirion.

Now this is interesting. Osiris' head surely 'talks'. Is it possible this head may have been the source of the information about the location of the head of Osiris (and perhaps something even more fantastic)? That is to say, did this pillar somehow communicate with Seti, letting him know its location? Is this why Seti kept this information secret, even from his architects? Were they constructing an observation (or listening) post beside the tomb of Osiris without even realizing it?

A possible reason why Seti would wish to keep the existence of the Osirion quiet is because the Osirion was a connection point to the gods of the First Time, an advanced civilization that vanished (approximately 10,000 B.C) due to a foreseen cataclysm.

The gods of the First Time are called the *Shemsu-Hor* (note the repetition of the name *Shem*). The Royal *Papyrus* of Turin (written during the time of Seti I's son Ramses II) records that the reign of the Shemsu-hor stretches to remote antiquity (up to a fantastic 40,000 years).[3] These kings lists call the Shemsu-Hor *Akhu*, meaning 'Transfigured Spirits'. Akhu or *Ax-hu* is the plural of *akh* or 'light', inferring that the Shemsu-Hor were light beings. I will refer to them as the Star Walking Illumined Ones or the Illuminati.

Robert Bauval speculates that the Shemsu-Hor were 'a lineage of real (and)... immensely powerful and enlightened individuals', masters of the science of astronomy, whose purpose was 'to bring fruition to a great cosmic blueprint'.[4]

"In the religious literature of Ancient Egypt," writes Andrew Collins, "they are said to have become the god's *mesniu*, 'workers of metal', or blacksmiths'".[5] The mesniu, says Barbara Walker, were *blacksmiths* or *alchemists* and priests of Isis.[7] Among other things, these angelic smiths fashioned weapons for Horus to maintain his supremacy.

The inference that is drawn here is that the Osiris Symbol (seen on p. 45) enshrined by Seti at Abydos originally belonged to the Shemsu-Hor. These Illumined Ones were the originators of this Pillar/Stimulator.

As a means to preserve its secrets, this civilization (Atlantis?) left artifacts, including, I suspect, an all-knowing Oracle. It is called the Head of Osiris. Seti had an image of this Power Tool of the Gods hung on the wall at Abydos. To uncover the secrets of the Illumined Ones we merely need to decode the Symbol of Osiris: the Oracle . (It appears the Cathars, the Templars and Bacon can be counted among those who have decoded it.)

On one wall of the Abydos temple Seti directed that the scribes produce a List of all the *Gods* who had ruled Egypt, long before the reign of men all the way back to the First Time. On the opposite wall, Seti I inscribed the names and regnal years of the pharaohs who had immediately preceded him. He omitted Akhenaton and his immediate successors (Smenkhkare, Tutankhamun, and Ay). This list is one of the most important in the world for the purposes of historical dating. It begins with the pharaoh Menkaure, 2532-2504 BC, who built the third pyramid at Giza.

So why did Seti omit Akhenaton? In a word the answer is control. Egyptologist E.A. Wallis Budge claimed that the means by which spiritual powers could be activated, i.e. the means by which the Cloak could be put on and one could become an Oracle, like Osiris, were coded by the Egyptian priesthood into the elaborate symbolism and ceremonies of the temples of ancient Egypt concerning Osiris. These powers were designed so that humanity could, one day, collectively share in their potentials by activating the Divine Force within. But, claims Budge, the 'higher' purpose of these teachings was lost after the Old Kingdom. The priesthood degenerated into a gang of sorcerers who ruled, controlled and manipulated the people under a beurocracy of gods.

Numerous researchers have claimed the period of darkness remained in place until the arrival of Akhenaton and Moses (who may be the same) *c.* 1400 B.C. Akhenaton attempted to overturn the buerocracy by implementing the religion of ATON, the One, eternal invisible Source, symbolized by the winged disk. Akhenaton's revolutionary teachings enabled all to embody the tone of life, and hence, to put on the Cloak, without the aid of the bureaucratic priesthood. Akhenaton's reign threw Egypt into chaos as he was declared the 'heretic' king and driven from power. His successor, Tutankhamun, was murdered. The old-time religion was restored.

Seti sought to wipe out all memory of this revolution.

It appears plausible to me that Seti did what a current era President might do upon the discovery of the secrets of the gods. He attempted to make use of them for himself, but covered them up or concealed them from his people. In fact, Seti I spoke of Osiris as the god who would destroy those who disobeyed him.[8]

The person that most embodied these secrets -- the man of light -- at the time was not Seti or even Akhenaton. It was Tutankhamun: the messiah of the Akhenaton Revolution.

As Ahmed Osmon has well documented, the life and death of the young Pharaoh Tutankhamun was decidedly "Messianic."[9] The literal meaning of the name Tutankhamun is "Living Image of the Lord (Tut - meaning likeness or image; Ankh - meaning life and symbolized by a cross; and amun - the god Amun)" He is described in his tomb as 'The Beautiful God, beloved, dazzling of face like the Aten...' However, the Lord that Tutankhamun's name now acknowledged was no longer the Aten, but Amun. It was switched because of political pressure from the Amen or Amun priesthood.

Following the trail of this king we are led to his throne. On the back of this magnificent chair is a beautiful blue apple out of which grows a blue lily.

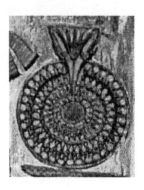

The back of his throne features a blue orb surrounded by rays. A blue lotus emerges from the blue orb. Is it the Blue Pearl?

153

Coptic (Egyptian) Christian depiction of a youth holding the ankh-cross and cluster of grapes. Fourth Century AD.

Fourteen hundred or so years later, the Essenes attempted to retrieve the teachings of Akhenaton and to recover the power of the Blue Pearl ◯ . The Early Coptic Christian fragment of a frieze, shown here, connects the ankh-cross of Akhenaton with the cluster of grapes. In Christian symbolism the cluster of grapes represents the 'head' of the Church. Christ was the "Stone from Heaven"[10] in whom was clustered all the fullness of the Godhead bodily!" It is He "of whom the whole family in heaven and earth are named".[11] "The Church, universally and locally, is a cluster of grapes. We are many yet one."

The fact that the *head of God* and the *cluster of grapes* are interchangeable symbols in Christian terms is enormously profound in its meaning to our investigation.

Mary Magdalene was associated in Christian myth with the severed head widely presumed to be the cranium of either Jesus or John the Baptist. Like the Egyptian *All*, we can now see that this is a symbol for the ultimate knowledge of the four Power Tools and for the Stimulator  of the Divine Particle .

As I have explored in previous books, especially *Blue Apples*, I believe this severed skull is a symbol for the Pillar once housed at Abydos and that this is a *skill*, the Wisdom of God, Sophia or Baphomet.

Possessing this skill, also symbolized by the cluster of grapes, transforms one into the Oracle and gives one the ability to open gateways in space and to *scale* the Ladder to Heaven ▛▜, the *Scala Dei* (in Latin).

These are the secrets stolen by the two spies, Joshua (Jesus in Greek) and Caleb, from the Anunnaki at Eschol ('the valley of the cluster, as in grapes) – i.e. E-*School* or E-*Skull*.

As far as the present work is concerned, the most important of all the *Skill* puns is revealed in the fact that

Sakla (Fool), another name for Yaldabaoth, is *SKL* without the vowels. When the vowels are reinserted and interchanged, *Sakla* is easily rendered as *Sakilla, Skilla...* or even *Skill A*.

In *Godseed: The Journey of Christ*,[14] Dr. Jean Houston presents what I consider a major revelation when she notes that *Christos* and *Chrestos* were interchangeable terms to the early Christians. *Chrestos* means simpleton, great *silly* or *blessed one*. She says that, in one of the apocryphal traditions, Pontius Pilate is supposed to have said to Jesus upon the Pillar, "*Ain Chrestos!*" or "You are the great silly."[15]

When the interchangeability between silly and skilly, both words mean "blessed," is taken into account, might Pilate have meant to say, "You are the great Chrestos or Skilly?" Did this mean "You are the Druid of great wisdom!" or "You are the great Blessed One!?" Paul affirms this notion that Jesus is the incarnation of the divine Wisdom when he says, "he is the power and the wisdom of God."[16] In John 10:19 Jesus said:

*"I am the **door**.*
*If anyone enters through **Me**, he shall be saved,*
and shall go in and out,
and find pasture."

Symbolically speaking, Paul's statement could read:

"he is the power ⊙ . He is the wise Oracle who spoke

156

the wisdom of God, ⚭ , through the Pillar ⚚ and
who opened the Way for us to pass through to the Pleroma.

An interesting line of 'head' stories accompanies the
story of Mary Magdalene. Cathar relics found in the
preceptory of Villeneuve, France, are said to have included
a hinged casket shaped like a woman's head. Reportedly
within the casket were two pieces of a female skull labeled
CAPUT LVIII (Head 58).

The Inquisitors were said to have found this head in the
Paris Temple, labeled Caput LVIII. This head is a shrine
containing some bones from a woman's head.

When the Templars were asked about this head, they
either said it was a Christian martyr woman, or it was *the
model of the speaking head that the pope Sylvester II made.*

Pope Sylvester II (d. 1003) was believed to have
possessed a golden head which spoke to him in oracles.
The Pope d'Aurillac, also known as Sylvester II, was most
famously known as the owner of a giant automaton oracle
head given to him by a magician with incredible power.
This mechanical head could answer any question posed to
it with a yes or no answer. A Spanish magician known as
the Black Moor programmed the oracle head. The Black
Moor is also said to be the author of *King Solomon's Key*,
an important occult text that had influenced Nostradamus
and Doctor John Dee. Sylvester II died in 1003, in a bizarre
murder plot just before ending the dark ages. The giant
oracle head has not been found. References still exist in the
Vatican library.

Inventor of Recursive Machines, Perpetual Motion Machines, Magic Staircases, Celestial globes, the Pendulum Clock, and Master of the Astrolabe, the genius d'Aurillac was also condemned as a dangerous madman and black magician. According to legend, his book of time was considered a dangerous, monstrous object, and if this infernal book were ever destroyed, the universe would be consumed along with it. Before d'Aurillac died he wrote a brief warning about reading the signs in the book called SYMBOSIS DESTINOS INFINITUM and buried the book deep within the catacombs underneath the Vatican.[17]

It is a well-attested fact that Pope Sylvester II was publicly accused by Cardinal Benno with being a sorcerer and an enchanter. The brazen "oracular head" made by his Holiness was of the same kind as the one fabricated by Albertus Magnus. The latter was smashed to pieces by Thomas Aquinas, not because it was the work of or inhabited by a "demon," but because the spook who was fixed inside, by mesmeric power, talked incessantly, and his verbiage prevented the eloquent saint from working out his mathematical problems. These heads and other talking statues, trophies of the magical skill of monks and bishops, were fac-similes of the "animated" gods of the ancient temples. One wonders if one these temples as the Serapeum of Alexandria. The accusation against the Pope was proved at the time. It was also demonstrated that he was constantly attended by "demons" or spirits.[18]

Francis Bacon, in my view, followed in the footsteps of Sylvester. To repeat, I believe the A **A** symbolism used by Bacon to identify his words connects him with the head of God transmission.

From his understanding of the secret information he had learned during his initiation into the Knights Templar concerning this head, I believe Bacon conceived the idea of reactivating various Secret Societies and in 1580 founded the secret Rosy Cross Literary Society in Gray's Inn. Later, such luminaries as Sir Isaac Newton would become Rosicrucians and set their sites on attaining invisibility.[19] He was among the Illumined Ones.

By far, Bacon's most intriguing work that contains references to the Pillar of the Oracle is the *New Atlantis*, a work of fiction that announced an allegorical vision for an illumined culture in America. It is an Illuminati Manifesto.

Fearing retribution from the power that seeks to block the efforts of investigators Bacon allowed the book to be published only after his death (in 1626).

In the story we visit the island of *BenSalem* (Solon of Salem, meaning 'Peace'). Saloman's House. The governor of the island meets the group and tells them a phenomenal story.

About twenty years after the ascension of their Savior the people of Renfusa (a city upon the eastern coast of the island) saw *a great pillar of light, a column, or cylinder, rising from the sea toward heaven*. On the top of it was seen a large cross of light, 'more bright and resplendent than the body of the pillar'.

At first, the people of the city watched the spectacle from the shore. As the scene grew more intense they sailed in boats to greet it. Sixty yards short of the marvelous pillar they found their boats were bound, they could go no further.

Among the chosen frozen was a wise man from the Society of Salomon's House, a college or temple described as "the Eye of this kingdom". Salomana, wrote Bacon, was the lawgiver of Atlantis.

Salomon contemplated the pillar of light for a while. At last, he fell to his knees, lifted his hands in prayer and spoke to the pillar floating on the water.

"'Lord God of heaven and earth; thou hast vouchsafed of thy *grace*, to those of our order to know thy works of creation, and true secrets of them; and to discern, as far as appertaineth to the generations of men, between divine miracles, works of nature, works of art and impostures, and illusions of all sorts."

In other words, the pillar of light Bacon is descrbing was a teacher of all the arts and sciences of civilization. The key to tracking this Atlantean knowledge, I suggest, is the head or the oracle, the 🜨 and 🜛 (which is the A **A**).

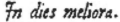

Note the A **A** in the center of this illustration and the Masonic term "Plus Ultra" ("more beyond") that appears on a banner between two pillars (representing Masonry) in an emblem from *Whitney's Choice of Emblems* (1586). Francis Bacon is said to have published this book.

The first Emblem in *Whitney's Choice* features the Pillar attached to the Ark.

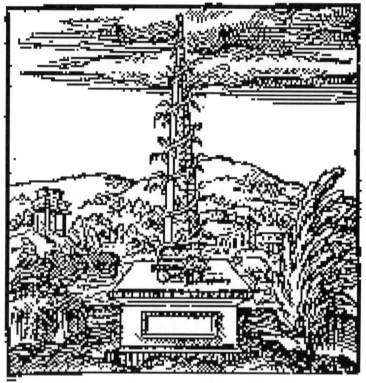

'*A mighty spire*' (or spear).

A mightie spyre, whose toppe dothe pierce the skie,
An ivie greene imbraceth rounde about,
And while it standes, the same doth bloome on highe,
But when it shrinkes, the ivie standes in dowt:
The Piller great, our gratious Princes is:
The braunche, the Churche: whoe speakes unto hir this.

These connections do not prove my thesis that Bacon possessed the Pillar of Osiris, but do, I believe, provide strong pictorial evidence that the secrets of this device were floating around Britain and France during his time.

Interestingly, in the *New Atlantis* Bacon tells how Salomon humbly beseeched the god in the pillar of light to give a sign.

Suddenly, Salomon's boat lurched toward the pillar. When he was close upon it the pillar and cross of light broke up, "and cast itself abroad, as it were, into a firmament of many stars, which also vanished soon after, and there was nothing left to be seen but a small ark or chest of cedar" that floated toward him, and contained a small green branch of palm. When the wise man hoised it into his boat, it opened, and there were found in it a book and a letter, both written in fine parchment, and wrapped in sindons of linen. The book contained all the canonical books of the Old and New Testament, according as you have them (for we know well what the churches with you receive), and the Apocalypse itself; *and some other books of the New Testament, which were not at that time written*, were nevertheless in the book.

In addition to references to unknown biblical texts, Bacon's *New Atlantis* is loaded with references to a futuristic technology.

"We procure means of seeing objects afar off, as in the heaven and remote places; and represent things near as afar off, and things afar off as near; making feigned distances. We have also helps for the sight far above spectacles and glasses in use; we have also glasses and means to see small and minute bodies, perfectly and distinctly; as the shapes and colors of small flies and worms, grains, and flaws in gems which cannot otherwise be seen, observations in urine and blood not otherwise to be seen. We make artificial rainbows, halos, and circles about light. We represent also all manner of reflections, refractions, and multiplications of visual beams of objects."

The summation of all the Baconian references allows us to suggest that Bacon was one in a long line of illumined ones who possessed the secret Gnostic gospels and familiarity with the talking head of the Oracle.

More detailed information on the A A symbolism of the Oracle is found in the story of Enki. We shall follow this trail in the next chapter.

9.
ENKI AND THE FLOWER OF LIGHT

Earlier, we noted that, among the Greeks, the light/dark Twins (the A **A**) were denominated *anake* (Annunaki), i.e. the *One Great Light*. In the Sumerian tradition, the drama of the twins was enacted by the half-brothers Enki and Enlil.

The assertion has been made that Enki and the Anunnaki created humans *in their image* as a slave race to mine gold ☉ (which is only half of the story, and is fact which suggests that the original seven Anunnaki could take on human form).

Mankind was also given the plough and hoe to work the land and *feed the gods*. From this start technology has been about the worship of the gods.

From the Gnostic perspective, the development of technology has been a massive human effort not only to feed the gods, but to become the gods.

E.A. sits before the plough, one of his inventions.

The hoe is quite provocative from a mythological point of view, spotlighting many linguistic and symbolic "coincidences" that convey hidden information about not only the creation of the human body, but also the A **A** symbol. For instance, the Egyptian ideograph for the *hoe* ⌐ is the letter 'A', A on its side, and is called MR (A*mer* or *AMOR*)![1] *Mer*, we have noted, means 'love' in Egyptian. The letter 'A' also symbolizes the plough ⅃ .[2]

As the hoe and ploughs are interchangeable, so too are hoes, ploughs and swords (which can be beaten into ploughshares). This interchangeability reflects, if not illuminates, the meaning of the black and white nature of

166

the A **A**. These secrets can be used to create peace or to conduct war. The choice is ours.

MR (*mister* or provider of *mist*) is a key mystery term.

MR is a Sumerian term for *brightness, shining*, as in Mar-Duk, the Bright One. (MR is the root of the name Nimrod or Ni-Meru-od). As Barbara Walker notes, Marduk claimed to have created the world by separating the celestial and the Abyssal waters, as Yaldabaoth did and as Yahweh (YHWH) did (Genesis 1:7).[3]

The Cathars called a vase or container MR the 'Flower of Light'.[4] It shows two serpents gathered at the head of the container topped by a fleur-de-lis.

One of the mysteries of Francis Bacon is the question of why he was baptized under the name Mr. Francis Bacon and not simply Francis Bacon.[5]

Interestingly, *Meru*, "the Thigh" is the name of the constellation known as the Great Bear (or Bier), the Celestial Ship of the North, the *Casket of Osiris*, and most provocatively, ***the Plough***.

Located in the Casket of Osiris (called *Nash*, 'the great coffin', by the Arabs)[5] are the galaxies M81 and M82, a bright UFO-shaped galaxy that sits 12 million light-years from Earth.

The spiral galaxy M81 (also called NGC 3031) is one of the most luminous galaxies in the Northern Hemisphere. It can easily be observed with small amateur telescopes and has even been seen with the naked eye by a handful of people. It is thought that an explosion at its center one and a half million years ago created the odd UFO shape,

At its center is a very bright nucleus. Researchers say the emissions from the region might represent a maturing black hole or, instead, could be the result of intense star formation and explosion, which would result in a phenomenon called a *starburst*.

"Starbursts are regions of intense and violent stellar activity where massive stars are being born and quickly go supernova," explains Alice Breeveld of the Mullard Space Science Laboratory (MSSL) at University College in London.[6]

M 82 and M 81 began colliding some 600 million years ago in a series of events that lasted about 100 million years. The study is discussed in the February 2001 issue of the *Astronomical Journal*.

According to Revelation, Jesus has a word of power written on his 'thigh'.[7] He wears many crowns (*rings?*).[8] He is clothed with a vesture dipped in blood.[9]

In my view there is a profound connection between the Word on the thigh of Jesus, his 'bloody' attire, the Pillar of Osiris and the Starburst in Seven Rays of Ursa Major.

The link is provided by the Egyptian artist who painted this illustration reproduced here. It is drawn from the rectangular zodiac carving which once graced the ceiling of the great temple Hathor at Denderah. It shows the first rays of the risen sun, Re or Horus (the Sun god) defeating the polar stars of Draconis and of the *Ursa Major*, the Plough.[10] The sunbeam or spear is pointed directly at the group of stars which we today call the Ursa Major or the Plough, but which the Egyptians called the *"Thigh"* or alternately the "Haunch of the Bull."[11]

The seven stars of the Plough, Ursa Major, shown as the Haunch of the Bull. From Denderah, Egypt.

The Egyptian sun-god Re *(Ray)* is an earlier version of the story of the Archangel Michael, the Dragon Slayer. He is here represented 'slaying the dragon' (the hippo was the 'dragon' of the Nile). The dragon in question could be the planet Tiamat, a former member of the Pleiades, known as the Seven Hathors to the Egyptians, which are found in the constellation Taurus the Bull. Or, it could be a reference to Yaldabaoth.

Pythagoras, one of the great inspirations to the Essenes, had a "Golden Thigh" ("Meru"). Again, this is either an impressive birthmark on his thigh, or Pythagoras possessed the secret of the golden Pillar or Casket of Osiris ⌐⌐, which we also know as the Golden Head, the Great A or the Plough. (Perhaps he used it to cultivate stardust from the collision of M81 and M82.)

Three centuries after Pythagoras the *Acts of Peter* includes the plough (*Meru, Su-Meru*) in the list of Jesus' titles. He is a plough maker.[12] Iranaeus' inspiration, Justin, lists the plough as interchangeable with *the cosmic cross*, the device that produces the Divine Force. Justin in turn derived his interpretation from primitive (Gnostic) Christian symbolism. The early Christians, in turn, derived their knowledge from Egypt, who got it from Su-Meru (the Plough) and Enki.

In describing Jesus as a maker of ploughs we don't seem to be talking about a farm or gardening tool. Rather, we are describing an instrument that, like a hoe, is a tool for cultivation of love. The plough we are talking about cultivates the Life Force Energy: a tone or a frequency; love (*mer, MR*), the vibration of life. The plough is the human body. The fruit that is cultivated is the ☿ .

170

In other books, particularly *God Making*,[13] I have presented evidence that Enki (E.A. or A-ya) created the human body as a resurrection machine, a ladder by which the soul could reach into the heavens and escape the rule of the Archons. It is a Tree of Life – a manufacturing *plant* -- that cultivates Blue Apples or Divine Particles ♏, ♉ .

Acting on the serpent's wise counsel, Adam and Eve ate of the fruit of the knowledge of good and evil (the Blue Apples or Blue Stones), and their eyes were opened to their incarceration. But before they could eat of the other tree which would break the Archons' power, Yaldabaoth (Enlil) intercedes and succeeds in keeping them captive, though no longer ignorant of their plight.

In the Judeo-Christian tradition Yahweh demotes the wise serpent to evil status, as Enlil demoted Enki, and evicts Adam and Eve from the Garden of Eden. At the gate of Eden ○ he places a flaming sword ✴ (the Sumerian symbol for the Anunnaki, according to French mystic symbolist Rene Guenon) with two cherubim on either side to guard it. This is the Fall (Phall) of man.

THE LIGHT BODY

According to a Rabbinic tradition, after the fall Yahweh (Enlil) clothed Adam and Eve in coats or garments of skin, not because of their nakedness, but *in exchange for their*

171

lost paradisiacal garments of light or bodies clothed with light originally made by Enki.[14]

The question of humanity's light body emerges from a Hebrew word play. The only difference between the Hebrew words for light and skin is one letter: **Aleph** (t) for light and **Ayin** (g) for skin. The Hebrew word for "Light" is "OR" (variant: 'ur) spelled "aleph vav resh" – **rut** (a way, pass, road or *route*, **rut**). The Hebrew word for "skin" is also "OR" (variant: *'or*), but is spelled "**ayin** vav resh" – **rug**.[15] (Remember, Hebrew words are read right to left).

In the metaphorical use *'or* signifies life over against death, Ps. 56:13. To walk in the "light" of the face of a superior, Prov. 16:15, or of God. Ps. 89:15, is an expression of a joyful, *blessed* (Skilled) life in which the quality of life is enhanced.

The letter Ayin (*eye in*) is represented by an *eye* and means to *see, know* or *experience*. Thus, when Adam and Eva ate the forbidden fruit (the Blue Apple) their *eyes were opened* and they began to *know* and *experience* good and evil. They also knew they were naked.

The idea of the open eye and the blossoming of human potential is central to the concept of the Oracle. In fact, it is embedded in the name Os-Iris.

The Bible gives us a reference in Matthew 6:22 "If your *eye be single your body will fill with light.*" Then we have the remark of Jacob in Genesis 32:30 "*I have seen* God face to face and I will call the place *Peniel.*"

Though *Peniel* is spelled differently then Pineal they are both pronounced the same, indicating the presence of an important word play or pun (*pala-y* or *pa-un*). The *Pineal*

172

Gland of the brain is a tiny bud of tissue located in the geometric center of the cranium (the center of the forehead between the two eyes) that secretes hormones to govern the nerves and biolocial cycle of the body. One of its most important secretions is melatonin, which sets our brain function level to sleep or awake.

The Pineal's shape, a pinecone is a double **PHI** spiral or two (S) O-phi-a spirals. **PHI** is the Divine Ratio, also called Golden Mean. This is expressed in the pentagon. The ratio of side to diagonal in any regular pentagon is the Golden Mean.

PHI derives from 5-sided symmetry. In two dimensions, this is a Pentagram -- the 'five lights', the seal of Solomon (Jedi-diah) and the ancient Greek Pythagorean School of Mathematics. Legends of Solomon's Temple retold by John Michell, an authority on ancient science, describe it as an instrument of a mystical, priestly form of alchemy by which *oppositely charged elements* in the Earth and atmosphere were brought together and ritually mated.[16] The product of the union was a 'spirit' that blessed and sanctified the people of Israel.[17] The marriage itself was technical, potentially dangerous and involved physics and astronomy.[18]

173

In three dimensions, five/PHI-sided symmetry is the

icosahedron and *dodecahedron* . As we will
explore momentarily, this is the symbol for Earth's
magnetic Grid and the Pleroma.

A five-pointed star with a dot, which Michell thinks
may represent Gulgotha, at its center and with the Hebrew
letters. J,R,S,L,M, is an ancient emblem for Jerusalem.[19]
Gulgotha, we recall, means 'the head', 'the stone' and 'the
gate'. It is an oracular center.

In my view, the piece of secret knowledge we are to
derive from the Pineal-Peneal pun is this. If God is light
and Jacob saw God face to face (at Peneal) because his
body was filled with light his Pineal Gland, which is the
body's light receptor, must have been active 'cloaking' his
body in a coat of many colors and preparing him for travel
into the other realms.

This is the Cloak or *Pallium* conferred upon Elisha by
Elijah just before his departure on a "chariot of fire" (2
Kings 2:11) that took him heavenward in a "whirlwind."
This appears to be a biblical code term for a vortex or a
stargate.

It is no coincidence that the word *Pallium* and Pleroma, ple-ro'-ma or Palla-Roma match so closely.

In the next chapter the time has come for us to look further into the Pleroma.

ORACLE OF THE ILLUMINATI

10.

THE GOD HEAD AND THE DODECAHEDRON

In my book *The A~tomic Christ*,[1] I presented evidence that beginning in the 1930s with President Franklin D. Roosevelt's quest for the secrets of Jesus in Mongolia, the US government has sought the sacred science or the Power Tools of the Oracle. In the book I presented evidence that the sacred science was used in the Manhattan Project.

If UFO researcher and super pilot John Lear is correct, immediately after this quest was conducted (1933-1935) several UFO crash recoveries were made including 'the big one' at Roswell, which became public knowledge.

According to a briefing Lear gave to radio talk show host Art Bell,[2] there were two survivors of the Roswell crash. Of these only one survived, passing in 1956. These beings were among a collection of 18 different alien species monitoring Earth. Some are good and some are hostile, says Lear, most are indifferent.

Coinciding with the theory of human origins put forth in Gnostic texts we have explored, Lear says that we found out (rediscovered?) that we are "the experimental product," "of an unknown alien race." We know them only by their messengers, the Greys, who are cybernetic organisms,

177

glorified robots, who work here at the behest of their employers monitoring us through abductions.

Lear claims the government was unable to find out what the experiment is all about except that the human body has been externally altered or corrected more than 60 times.

And most insightful of all to our study, the aliens refer to us as "Containers."

There's been speculation, says Lear, that the souls our bodies contain is the reason for the experiments. But nothing's been proven or determined.

However, as we have seen, the Gnostic Christians shared a similar worldview concerning our bodies.

All we need to do is substitute the word "Grey" for "archon" and we have the essential Gnostic story of the creation of humanity.

Exo-politics (or the politics of alien affairs) is not the only area where humanity made strides in reclaiming ancient knowledge of the Oracle.

In *The Day After Roswell*, former Pentagon official, Col. Philip J. Corso, (Ret.), revealed his personal involvement in the handling of artifacts from the crash of a UFO at Roswell.[3] He claims the US government reverse-engineered military technology, including a particle beam weapon, from the downed disk and "seeded" alien technology to a Who's Who of American military contractors.

At the turn of the 21st century we are living in a New Atlantis made possible by the technology of beings the ancients called Archons, Ruler or the gods.

While this statement may seem hyperbolic to some, there is no question that in the 20th century, physics made enormous mental leaps in revealing the secrets of the Oracle, i.e. the inner nature of the "veil" that separates us from the science of stargates and interphasic travel, teleportation or quantum entanglement as it is known today. These developments took us down the rabbit hole of abstract mathematical systems into an alien world that shattered common-sense preconceptions about the nature of things. There is no direct evidence that this science came from aliens. I do feel, however, that a strong case is being made for this origin by numerous researchers. Compelling evidence is also being presented that traces usage of this same science to the ancient world.

In the early 20th century the newly (re)discovered phenomenon of radioactivity, Rutherford's experiments in atomic transmutation and Marie Curie's breakthroughs in radiation, may well have represented the return of the ancient science of the Roman god Mercury or Mari-cury.

Einstein's Relativity theory (1905), which introduced the modern world to the paradoxical ideas on the nature of time, and the quantum theory with its sea of probabilities,

in which an electron is simultaneously a wave ,

and a particle or dot •, seemed light years removed from the comfort of the metaphysical Kansas of the past several hundred years. However, as our investigation into Gnostic symbols has shown, Jesus and the early Gnostic Christians may have applied and encoded this theory.

Since Einstein, physicists have been pursuing a Holy Grail theory to unite the *four fundamental forces of nature* (the four evangelists) within one common mathematical structure, a Unified Field Theory or Theory of Everything (TOE). Such a theory would answer questions like: How did the universe begin? What is the origin of time? What is the secret of time travel? Various ideas were proposed -- Super-symmetry, String theory, the idea that a particle was actually a tiny super quantum string that both vibrates at specific frequencies (like a guitar or *kitara* string) and rotates in a ten-dimensional space. 'Kansas' suddenly vanished and a 'new' matrix appeared.

Beginning in the 1970s a crisis emerged in physics as it burst through a threshold in the alien world into a realm of speculative super metaphysics. Simply, the advanced theories of the brightest minds of modern physics have little direct connection with anything that can be empirically measured. It's pure speculation (some would call pseudoscience). There can be no experiments conceivable to test these elegant theories. The energies required are staggeringly high. We are still decades away before human beings can harness enough energy to perform the quantum gravity experiments that need to be done to make us a Type II civilization. The present generation of particle accelerators (an immensely powerful knife that cuts matter into quarks and reveals the forces that drive them), though they are considered the most complex experimental tools ever built, are thought to be billions of times less powerful than the energies required to test the theories of quantum gravity which unite the four fundamental forces. Quantum theory, notes Nobel Prize winning physicist Leon

Lederman, "demands more and more powerful accelerators to study smaller and smaller things."

The problem is further complicated, observes science writer David Peat, by the fact that the theories presented by today's "post modern physics" are so far removed from our ordinary reality, so abstract and so advanced that they cannot even describe to one another the theories with our present mathematical and symbolic language systems.[4] To paraphrase David Peat, it's like trying to explain Eddie Van Halen's electric guitar sound in words.

All physicists (who must feel like they were born a hundred years too soon) can do to test the cosmological consequences of their theories is to test their consistency and their interrelationship with other theories of the universe.

In other words, as a result of the light speed technological progress we have achieved since the 1950's we have encountered the ring pass not. The "great dream" is to pass through this ring. In order to do so, I believe, we must contact the God Head for the next clue as to how to harness the power of our galaxy.

Meanwhile, as physicists searched for the TOE, metaphysicians and psychologists, including Swiss psychiatrist Dr. Carl G. Jung, sought the secrets of synchronicity and a psychological theory of everything to explain meaningful coincidence. Jung is also the first scientist to seriously study UFOs.

Between 1912 and 1926, Jung delved into a study of Gnosticism and early Christianity. He found in Gnosticism an early, prototypical depth psychology. He believed that Christianity, and as a result Western culture, had suffered because of the repression of Gnostic concepts. Gnosis leads to connecting with the inner Oracle and the God Head. In looking for ways to reintroduce Gnostic ideas to modern culture, Jung found them in alchemy and in a sequence of 12 operations.[5]

Jung defined synchronicity as the co-incidence in time of two or more causally unrelated events which have the same meaning. Jung's definition infers that certain events in the universe cluster together by a force that operates outside of the normal laws of science. They represent the transcendent, unseen hand of God operating in our lives. (Critics claim Jung suffered from a mental disorder known as *apophenia*, the spontaneous perception of connections and meaningfulness of unrelated phenomena.)

Synchronicity theory flew in the face of cause and effect physics, which sees the universe as a string of events with each event arising from the event before it. In this theory we are all rather like a person walking through a hall of doors. As we open one door it opens into another hall and another door, ad infinitum. Jung's theory takes us above the hall itself and looks for the cause of the door's opening from outside the hallway. It is intended to help us make contact with the Source.

Synchronicities, notes David Peat, were crucial to the concept of history in ancient China.[6] Contrary to the West's view that all historical events are strictly the end result of cause and effect, Chinese history was viewed in terms of the cluster of events that coincidentally happened to occur together in time. Omens were recorded along with military expeditions. According to Hellmut Wilhelm, son of the famous translator of the *I Ching*:

"The interplay of forces that determine a historical moment sounds a chime... only by concentrating on this sound and yielding to it may we recognize its essence and its effect."[7]

In the Eastern view an event is unique and individual, but is also the manifestation of a greater order. This greater order, the key to Jung's theory of synchronicity, was the *Pleroma*, the "God Head" out of which all reality is born.[8] The *International Standard Bible Encyclopedia* provides this translation of pleroma, which is generally, but not invariably, rendered *"fullness"* in the New Testament. Etymologically, pleroma -- which itself is derived from the verb *pleroo*, "I fill" (a pun on I fool) -- signifies "that which is or has been filled"; it also means "that which fills or with which a thing is filled"; then it signifies "fullness," "a fulfilling."

The 'real' psycho-physical world we inhabit is a copy of the higher perfect order of the Pleroma. This synchronistic intelligence holds the world together. The Oracle is the one who can connect with this Source and fill the body with its light. They are the bridge between Heaven and Earth. In synchronicity theory the bridge does not have

to go far. The distance between objects becomes zero, ◯ ,

the distance between events becomes zero, ◯ , and

everything occurs synchronistically .

In *Christianity and Evolution* the French Christian mystic Tielhard de Chardin amplifies the notion of Pleroma and focuses on the power of synchronicity to create *a mystical body.*[9]

"... *consummated mystical body* (that is, the Pauline pleroma). In the first place, since the pleroma is the kingdom of God in its completed form ..."[10]

"... *the contact* [with Christ] which is to ensure their integration into the pleroma."[11]

"To love one's brothers and to receive the body of Christ ... is organically to build up, element by element, the living unity of the pleroma in Christ."[12]

"The Incarnation ends in the building up of a living church, of *a mystical body*, of a consummated totality, of a pleroma ..."[13]

"The pleroma = *the mystical body*."[14]

THE DODECAHEDRON

In order to make our quest for the secrets of the Blue Star of the Pleroma work, that is, in order to build the bridge, we will need the knowledge encoded in what I term the key to the Pleroma, the dodecahedron.

In his discourse *Phaeado*, 'Plato' – the nickname of Ari-Stocles (about 427–347 B.C.), the aristocratic Athenian oracle who reintroduced the story of Atlantis to the modern mind -- makes an astonishing observation that reveals the logo of the Oracle.

If you could see it from above, he says, "the *true* Earth," "like the inner Earth," looks like the balls that are made of twelve pieces of many-colored leather.

A twelve-patched leather ball describes a dodecahedron

(from *dodeca*, twelve, and *hedron*, a base or fortification) a solid with 12 pentagonal faces and 20 vertices.

It is fascinating in the extreme that Plato (A-palo, the sun god, gave his name to A-Pala-to) would make such an astonishing observation.

Where did Plato get the inspiration to describe Earth as a three-dimensional pentagonal web into which the soul incarnates? Did he have some means of traveling into our Blue Apple's orbit to make such a statement?

Did he learn it from some secret sect of initiates? Or did he 'download' it from the collective consciousness?

Many are familiar with the Platonic solids. Plato, the disciple of Pythagoras, ascribed shapes to the miniscule particles that form the four elements of matter:

Earth

Air   Fire

Water

To the mysterious fifth element he ascribed the dodecahedron.

ORACLE OF THE ILLUMINATI

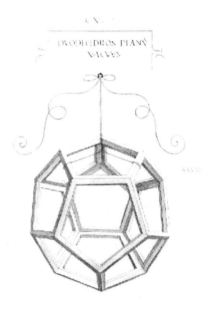

*Leonardo da Vinci, the quintessential Renaissance man,
drew this dodecahedron.*

Pythagoras says that ...

the earth is made from the cube,
fire from the pyramid,
air from the octahedron,
water from the icosahedron,
and the sphere of the whole (the Aither) from the
dodecahedron.

This fifth essence is the *quintessence*, called the *living
spiritual energy, the Holy Light, the Holy Spirit, Sophia,*

the Divine Force and *the Atomic Universal Mother* (AUM,

◯ 〜〜) or *thought substance* of which the *World* is composed. In the East it is called *Wood* and is symbolized

by the three orbs ♉ of the Trinity, the *Word* ('*Love*') in the New Testament.

Our souls are like fish in a Sea of Glass swimming around in search of this 'watery' substance, called *Akasha* (*Acacia* is another name for the Wood), that takes the form of everything we see, feel or otherwise experience. This glass window through which I peer at this very moment is but a manifestation of this substance. So am I. The Oracle is a master of this substance. But, what is it?

Yes. What *is it*? was the name given to the *manna* that fell from Heaven by the Israelites. Leading researchers, including Laurence Gardner, have presented a well worked-out theory that manna is a code term for a secret monatomic superconducting substance used by the ancients in space-time manipulation. Akhenaton, among others, manufactured this superconductive monatomic gold at a temple-manufacturing plant at Serabit E-Khadim in the Sinai. This substance fed the light body of the Pharaoh and provided a key to the Holy *Field of the Blessed*. I believe Akhenaton used the Oracular Cosmic G-Spot Stimulator technology referenced at Abydos in this process.

Physicists call this light substance "dark or black matter" because it is hidden, occult. Ninety percent of the matter in the universe is unaccounted for and remains elusive to detection. The existence of this dark matter has led to speculation of the existence of particles or species or entities made of matter, which can attain velocities faster than the speed of light.

"God made use of it when he painted the universe," wrote Plato in his dialog *Timaeus*.

Plato (and Leonardo) would have celebrated the cover of *Nature* magazine from October 8, 2003. An article published in *Nature* announced that the universe could be shaped like a soccer ball, a dodecahedron.

Nature magazine, October 8, 2003.

If the universe is shaped like a dodecahedron, all the forms that appear in it would be a repackaging of this shape, including you and I. This is the "pattern" mentioned in *The Hypostasis of the* Archons: "And she established each of his offspring in conformity with its power – *after the pattern of the realms that are above, for by starting from the invisible world the visible world was invented.*"

When the Hebrews said we were made in the image of God it meant we were made of this thought substance, the

Word from the God Head . Today, dodecahedron shaped nanoassemblers may be the key to creating a new world at the nano level.

Following the As above. So Below law the earthly Matrix is a miniature of the cosmic Matrix. Plato appears to have recognized the dodachedron's role in the creation of his world.

His description suggests there is a hidden energetic component – a 12-angled Planetary Grid or Matrix – that surrounds the Earth. As we follow the thread of the number twelve we are led into a rich net of associations that shine like metaphysical gems.

The Tree of Life had 12 fruits. The breastplate of the Hebrew head-priest, the Oracle, had 12 stones. Twelve is the number of constellations, tribes, and apostles.

A key connection between the Ladder to Heaven and the number 12 is found in the Genesis story of Jacob's ladder. At *Luz* ('light' or 'almond') Jacob lay his head on a *stone* and saw a ladder with angels on either side.[16] He ascended this ladder to a heavenly realm. Upon his return he declared the spot of real estate (the oracle) a "blessed gate to Heaven." [17]

In Genesis 28:18 he then set up a pillar (a Cosmic G-Spot Stimulator?) on the spot and poured *oil* upon it.

There were Twelve Tribes of Israel who were the 12 sons of Jacob. Following the 'As Above. So Below' law when Jacob gave his blessing to his twelve sons, he was referring not only to twelve individuals, but to the

development of twelve attributes to be awakened within in the human soul (by the Oracle). These paralleled the twelve characteristics of the twelve signs of the zodiac, the star gate.[18] The work of these twelve sons dominated most of the Old Testament. Each tribe expressed the qualities of one sign of the zodiac and responded to a certain number. No tribe was wholly good or bad. These twelve signs and their corresponding numbers are operative in the lives of every individual, for each person indeed is a miniature universe.

Another excellent example of how the dodecahedral symbolism is hidden with the symbolism of the Israelites is the story of Aaron, the Hebrew Oracle.

A A RON THE ORACLE

In approximately 1400 B.C. Aaron ('the Enlightened' or 'the Illumined'), Moses's brother, had been initiated into the ancient Sumerian and Egyptian mysteries of the Oracles. This is evidenced by the device, which Aaron wore along with the Garment of Glory of the Head Priest, called the *Essen* or *Breastplate of Righteousness and Prophecy*. Inside the Essen Aaron was told to place the "Urim and Thummim".[19] This device was made of 12 stones. Josephus called it 'the Oracle' and is said to resemble the Earth. This description is a hint that we are talking about the dodecahedron.

The precision with which the Israelites crafted the cloak of *Aaron* ('light', 'enlightened') in preparation for his meetings with the Lord,[20] reveals that it served an important function. It *filled* him with the Holy Spirit, says Exodus.[21] (In Gnostic terms, it connected him with the fullness of the Pleroma.) We know that Aaron wore this cloak when he tended the Ark of the Covenant. Aaron's cloak operated in conjunction with the Ark.

In addition to the breastplate, this suit featured a *blue* ephod with gold wires interwoven in it, and a robe, an embroidered coat, a mitre, and a girdle.[22] Pomegranates (balls, apples) of blue, of purple, of scarlet hung from the hem. A crown or "miter" (modeled after the fish headed priests of E.A.) was to be worn on top of the head.

The vestments of the High Priest make more than a fashion statement. They symbolize the four levels or elements within a human being. The outer *blue* ephod, with its golden wiring, represents the Divine part of a man (Azilut), with the blue surcoat as a heavenly or spiritual aspect (Beriah). The under garment represents the souls (Yezirah), and the priest's own body is the physical vessel, container or temple. The task of the Illumined one is to bring all these 'wheels' or 'levels' into a harmonious vehicle, in order to become a being in whom – as in the

Head Priest – the universe and Divinity are consciously manifest and speak to the people.

In reading the Old Testament we get the impression that the Urim and Thummim figure as part of the equipment of the High priest, functioning in conjunction with the ephod. (In other words it was a part of the Cloak of Light or the Cloak of the Illi or Illuminati.) In special circumstances the Bible refers to the Ephod as having oracular ability.[23] So closely are their functions matched that they appear to be one and the same thing. The oracular function is reinforced by the Hebrew word for the breast pocket in which the Urim and Thummim were contained, *hoshen hammishpat*, which means "the breastplate of the *oracular* decision."

The Urim and Thummim are among the most unique objects in all myth and Scripture, in that it appears humans did not make them. Unlike the Ark of the Covenant and the Cloak of Aaron, the method of the construction of these sacred objects is not detailed nor is a clear description provided of their appearance.

The meanings of the words in Hebrew are Thummim (perfections), and Urim (lights), rendering them/it as *Perfect Light*. Although this *Perfect Light* is referenced several times in the Old Testament, there is an aura of darkness about it, as no one over the intervening several thousand years can say to what it referred, save for the fact that it was some sort of instrument through which Aaron could communicate with Yahweh and receive his encrypted decisions and which translated languages.[24]

When functioning this oracle apparently emitted light. This conclusion is supported by the report of Josephus in his *Antiquities of the Jews*, Book III, chapter 8, section 9, where he mentions:

"...yet will I mention what is still more wonderful than this: for God declared beforehand, by those 12 stones which the High Priest bare on his breast, and which were inserted into his breastplate, when they should be victorious in battle; *for so great a splendor shone forth from them before the army began to march*, that all the people were sensible of God's being present for their assistance... now this breastplate, and this sardonyx, left off shining 200 years before I composed this book, God having been displeased at the transgressions of his laws."

The 'shining' aspect of the Urim and Thummin suggests either a radiance, which indicates electricity, or an illumination, wisdom, in which case I would suggest the light is blue.

Many believe the Urim and Thummim gave yes or no answers. The people would ask Aaron a question to be answered by God, through the Ark. Aaron would stand before the inquirer, and then would enter the holy of holies of the Tabernacle (the room where the Ark was held).

Attempts have been made to connect them to the Babylonian Tablets of Destiny or Stones of Enlightenment. As we investigate these Tablets or Stones we find an important connection to Sophia that can be applied to the Urim and Thummim.

Also known as the ME (pronounced *may*), the Babylonian word for "mother-wisdom" these oracular tablets are cognate with the Sanskrit *medha*, feminine wisdom, and Egyptian Stone of *met* or *Maat* ('Truth'). In Gnostic terms, the ME are the Stones of Sophia.

Though neither their construction nor their appearance has ever been described, if we speculate that the Urim and Thummim (s)*tones* are the twin male and female serpents -

-               ,   and   -- ancient Hindu mythology may have vital cosmic associations for Urim and Thummim. Along with the icosahedron the dodecahedron represented male and female powers respectively. The Icosahedron has 20 faces and 12 vertices while the Dodecahedron has 12 faces and 20 vertices, an exact reciprocal of each other.

To me it would make sense that one of the stones used to communicate with God would be shaped like God.

Edgar Cayce concurred with biblical experts who speculated the Urim and Thummin were *blue stones*, although he thinks the were possibly lapis,[25] long considered the stone of the gods.

I am nonetheless encouraged by Cayce's conclusion, as this would align the Urim and Thummim with the Blue Pearl and the Blue Apple.

11.
THE STAR WALKER

In the second century AD, the Gnostics picked up on Plato's idea and described the sphere of Earth being surrounded by a 12-angled pyramid. These 12 angles are described as "eyes", "pipes," and even more fascinating to our story, as "holes" in the Earth.[1] It is probable they were also influenced by the Egyptians, who said a serpent called *Chnoubis* or *Kanobis* ('wisdom') guarded these holes.

The Oracle is the place where the mighty heavenly waters meet the Earth.

"The miracle," said John Lilly, "is that the universe created a part of itself to study the rest of it, and that this part in the studying itself finds the rest of the universe in its own natural inner realities."

The pentagonal face of the dodecahedron refers us to ancient legends of the *Perfect Man,* for the star born within the dodecahedron's pentagon is the configuration of Cosmic Man, says Robert Lawlor in his book *Sacred Geometry*. This is the perfector of life, the Golden

Proportion .[2]

195

This is the god star, or golden gate, 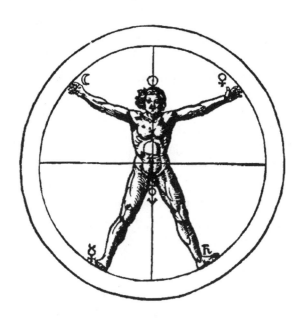 , to the Oracle through which the Essenes believed Christ would enter. (It is also the logo of Pythagoras who cut an apple in half to reveal this pattern.)

Pentagrammic man from Cornelius Agrippa De Occulta Philosophia, 1534.

In Egypt the *etheric* or *quintessence* was represented in

the form of the five-pointed **sba** star, , which is a keystone oracular hieroglyphic. It therefore is striking that the *pentagrammic man* should reappear today in the form of the *Pentagon's* super man (the MIT *e*-Man).

Sba or *Sa Ba* is an important oracular term. So let's look at it closely. To begin, *Sba* is the Egyptian term for *star*, *star god*, and *door*,[3] as well as *to teach, to learn, to instruct*.[4] It is used as *Seb*, to *pass through* (Yaldabaoth,

),[5] and in the name   *Sabala*, from the Central Asian myth of Mount Meru, the world axis, and *Shambhala*.

When we drill into the meanings of this word we discover that in ancient Egyptian the *Ba* element of Saba means *soul*. In Egypt, the *ka* was considered the soul's *twin light body*. Every human being has a 'lower self' (the *ba*) and an immortal Higher Self (*ka*). The lower self resides in the physical body. The Higher Self resides in Heaven. It is closest to God. Plato taught that this twin was our Guardian Spirit.[6]

The *purified ones* (Cathars) were shown with *outstretched* arms like the pentagrammic man. Esoteric writers claim this indicated that they were 'dead'. Dead is a pun for 'true' as in 'dead on' -- meaning they were in their True Blue Etheric or Light bodies again.

Buddha and Arhat.

Jesus hands off to a mirror image of himself.

In the woodcut shown here from Rennes, France Jesus demonstrates this process. He lifts his arms to a mirror image or twin of himself that exists in an exalted state. Note the 'dead head' or skull, the symbol of Sophia and the Oracle, at the base of his feet.

I have also shown that this body posture was used as a prayer posture through which the *Ba* contacted the *Ka* and drew down the essence of heaven that transformed the lower self into the Higher Self. This heavenly essence is called the *baa*.

Robert Temple traces the meaning of *ba* to the Egyptian *baa*, 'metallic substance'. Another provocative meaning of *baa*, which fits perfectly with our inquiry, is '*the material of which heaven is supposed to be made*'.[7]

This material is the quintessence  milled from the 

Important insight into the outstretched arms  code is found in the burial chamber of the Tomb of Ramses VI. On the north wall is the mysterious *Book of Aker*, the *Book of Light*.[8] According to the myth, *Nut*, the Galactic Core (or Nut) of our Milky Way galaxy, swallows the sun each evening and gives birth to it each morning, 'younger than it was the evening before'. The mystery of this re-*Generation* is the subject of the *Book of Ak-er* and of Gnostic teaching.

The concept of re-*Generation* through a prayer posture links with the Cloak of Light. In ancient times the robes of the Head Priest, the Oracle of the Order of Melchizedek, were called the "Garments of Glory," for, says Manly P. Hall, they resembled the regenerated and *spiritualized* nature of man.[9] From this we connect the Cloak with the Oracle with the prayer posture.

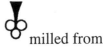

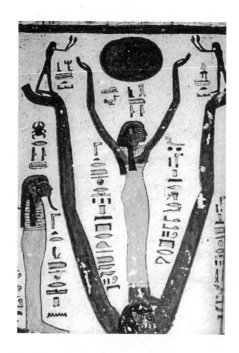

Detail from the Tomb of Ramses VI, c. 1150 BC. The outstretched arms of the sun goddess hold the energy or light (Ak) of the Core.

Moses demonstrated this power of re-*Generation* for us. The Bible tells us that in his battle with the Amalek Moses' hands grew heavy, and the Israelites took a *stone* and put it under him, and *Hur* and *Aaron* held Moses' arms outstretched.[10]

Through this body posture -- the Y -- Moses served to create a conducting channel for the inflow of the power of the Holy Spirit to aid the Hebrews in (t)winning their battle against darkness (ignorance). While Moses assumed this body posture, Joshua was victorious over the Amalek.

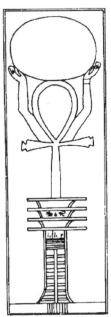

Atlas holds the 'world' on his broad shoulders.

Plato's nickname means 'the broad one', and was an allusion to his broad shoulders. He was a 'Mighty Man' in the model of Atlas, the priest-king of Atlantis who lifted the world on his powerful shoulders, a conduit between Earth and Heaven, material and nonmaterial. Within the Hall of the octagonal Globe Theater where Shakespeare's plays were performed stood a figure of Atlas bearing the

Sphere on his back, a further emblem, or speaking picture, proclaiming the same truth. Hieroglyphics and ciphers in many forms were much in vogue in Bacon's day.

As the picture of the statue on the previous page reveals, Atlas did not lift the physical world. He lifted the 'Word', the ether, the spiritual energy upon which the 'world' is built represented by the zodiac.

The assistance of *Hur* and *Aaron* when Moses invoked this body posture to channel the Holy Spirit (Sophia) is essential code. Together, my muse whispers, their names spell Hur-Aaron or simply '*heron*', the name of the 'Bird of Light' of Egyptian symbolism. Along with the hawk the heron symbolized rebirth as a being of light to the Egyptians. The heron symbolism is interchanged with the phoenix. In early Christian tradition the phoenix -- **PHI**-nix or (P)*hoe*-nix -- was adopted as being resurrection and immortality.

According to Manly P. Hall, the Egyptians occasionally represented the phoenix as having the body of a man and the wings of a bird. This avian creature had a tuft of feathers upon its head and its arms were upraised in an attitude of prayer. As the phoenix was the symbol of regeneration, the tuft of feathers on the back of its head might well symbolize the activity of the pineal gland, or third eye, the occult function of which was apparently well understood by the ancient priest-craft.[11]

The Phoenix or bird-man. Manly P. Hall. He sits on the Egyptian hieroglyph for NEB, meaning 'Lord'.

Many ancient cultures believe through meditation and visualization, you can stimulate the pineal gland to function as it has for our ancestors – as a generator of the Blue Apple or the Blue Being. As noted, Hindu mystics practicing Kundalini yoga strive to cause the spirit fire to rise up the spinal cord and feed the crown chakra, igniting a halo around the head. Ancient Egyptian royalty, such as Akhenaton, wore the coiled cobra over the third eye to symbolize the Kundalini or 'eye of Horus' had been awakened in them.

Akhenaton with the cobra at his third eye.

The great teachers say it is possible for the student or disciple to raise Kundalini up to the third eye on effort alone (spontaneous eruptions are also reported), but to raise it *through* the pineal, or third eye, is not possible without the help of the guru, the Blue Being. Kundalini, when it

205

reaches the third eye, vibrates through the pineal like a waving finger or tail. Some report that at one stage of the rising Kundalini, they can see and feel this fluctuating finger along with an *intense buzzing*. Researcher Itzhak Bentov, who approached the mysteries of Kundalini through studies of the effects of vibration on human physiology, wrote a classic work on this subject, *Stalking the Wild Pendulum*. About this vibrating he says, "When something moves so fast that it uses almost no time for its movement then it moves at an almost infinite speed, and when something is going so fast, then it must be present at all places at once!...:omnipresence."[12] So this vibration of the pineal, created by the ascended Kundalini sets up a communication system with the universe. The pineal is a radio receiver for the God Head. In this Cathar symbol the

wisdom ⋀⋀ is in the head ⟨symbol⟩ with two eyes. It is combined with the cross, the symbol of ascent or the ladder to God ⟨symbol⟩ , ⟨symbol⟩ .

Bentov's observations (using ballistocardiogram) of the seated subject engaged in deep meditation reveal a rhythmic *sine wave* pattern. He attributes this to the development during the course of meditation of a 'standing wave' in the aorta, the main artery from the heart, that is reflected in rhythmic motion of the body. This resonating oscillator - - the heart aorta system -- in turn 'entrains' further bio-oscillators -- the brain, the cerebral ventricles and the sensory cortex of the brain -- which together effect a modification of the cerebral magnetic field. This co-ordinated system activates a traveling stimulus, an oscillating 'current', in the sensory cortex tissue, which is finally polarized to a point where each hemisphere of the brain produces a pulsating magnetic field. Bentov writes:

'This magnetic field -- *radiated by the head acting as an <u>antenna</u>* -- interacts with the electric and magnetic fields already in the environment. We may consider the head as simultaneously a transmitting and receiving antenna, tuned to a particular one of the several resonant frequencies of the brain.' Bentov suggests that the 'kundalini' effect may be regarded as part of a development of the <u>nervous system</u>: 'We can postulate that our magnetic 'antennae' will bring in <u>information</u> about our extended system -- the planet and the sun -- and will allow us to interpret geophysical phenomena and signals to better advantage.'"[13]

THE PINEAL AND DMT

From 1990-1995 Dr. Rick Strassman conducted cutting-edge clinical research at the University of New Mexico in search of a biological basis of spiritual experience.[14] He focused his research on the pineal gland. His studies revealed that it is a producer of the chemical

DMT, one of the most powerful psychedelics known. Plants also manufacture this hallucinogenic chemical or "spirit molecule" as Strassman terms it. It consistently produces near-death and mystical experiences, including startling encounters with intelligent nonhuman beings (possibly "aliens"). Subjects frequently reported making "contact" and dialoging with "guides" and "helpers" from the nonmaterial realms. DMT is certainly a qualified contender for the trigger of the Blue Apples or Blue Stones of the Oracle. One detail of the DMT experience is most intriguing. Subjects reported a *humming sound* or an *intense pulsating-buzzing sound and vibration* that preceded the appearance of "alien" humanoid beings who were "gatekeepers".[15] One subject described these entities *pouring communication* into him. Another described them as "cloaked", like silhoutettes.[16] They operated technology or machinery.

Complimentary to Dr. Strassman's research are the findings of influential psychiatrist John Mack who has published several key works on the alien abduction phenomenon.[17] His description of the abduction experience has several important parallels with the DMT experience. As the abduction begins, Mack says, "consciousness is disturbed by a *bright light, humming sounds, strange bodily vibrations* or paralysis... or the appearance of one or more humanoid or even human-appearing strange beings in their environment." Mack highlights the sense of *high-frequency vibrations* many abductees report. So powerful is this experience, reports Mack, it makes abductees feel as if they are coming apart at the molecular level.

Some abductees report that the experience of having instant transfer of massive amounts of information downloaded through some form of neuropsychological programming. Abductees explain the alien language as a universal language of visual symbols, instead of words or sounds.

Two important common elements, perhaps links, between the DMT experience and the "abduction" experience is that *the beings appear to envy our embodiment* and *the subjects feel the experience is transformation and spiritual that provides a feeling of connectedness with all of creation.*[18]

Strassman's and Mack's inspired research will help open the way toward a fuller understanding the pineal and DMT and will push the boundaries of science and spirituality.

In addition to DMT, another psychoactive (an illegal) substance is Ketamine, widely used as an animal tranquilizer by veterinarians. At lower doses it has a mild, dreamy feeling similar to nitrous oxide (laughing gas). Users report feeling floaty and slightly outside their body. Numbness in the extremities is also common. Higher doses of "Special K" produce a hallucinogenic (trippy) effect, and may cause the user to feel very far away from their body. This experience is often referred to as entering a "K-hole" and has been compared to a near death experience with sensations of rising above one's body. Many users find the experience spiritually significant, while others find it frightening. It can be extremely dangerous.

Reading the following description of a Ketamine

experience reveals details that are, by now, quite familiar to us.

"I lay down, and within two or three minutes the now familiar onset of the Ketamine overtook me; *a loud ringing in my ears*, followed by a narrowing/contraction of my reality tunnel until the outside world and my physical body were utterly gone. Then, instead of the usual complete merge with pure consciousness, I found myself as a bodiless point of awareness and energy floating in the midst of what seemed to be a vast vaulted chamber. There was a sense of presence all around, as though I was surrounded by millions of others, although no one else could be seen. In the center of the chamber was *a huge, pulsing, krishna-blue mass of seething energy that was shaped in a geometric, mandalic form.* I had the sense that I had somehow stumbled into the blast furnace at the heart of the cosmos, the engine that drives the process of creating manifest reality out of the thoughts of the mind of god. It was pulsing at a steady pace, and emitting sound vibrations (which sounded remarkably like chanted "Om's") as it pulsed that instantly crossed a synesthetic line from something heard to an object beheld, much like McKenna's descriptions of the language of the elves he encounters in DMT space."[19]

Advances in neuroscience have recently provided us with new insights as to the mechanisms involved at the mind-brain interface.

Another series of studies carried out since 1985 has involved the mulberry shaped crystalline deposits in the Pineal. Recently, however, a study led by Sydney Lang and carried out in Israel using scanning electron microscopy described the presence of a new form of small geometric shapes which the discoverers have called "brain dust." Reasons for the formation of the cubic, hexagonal and cylindrical microcrystals and their possible biological significance is not known at this time. The crystals are calcite. However, since the crystals exhibit piezeoelctric properties, researchers have speculated that *a coupling mechanism to external electromagnetic fields* is possible.[20]

This may be the "brain sand" of the alchemists.

The drug-induced NDE, and the alien abduction phenomenon, is of considerable importance to medicine, neuroscience, neurology, psychiatry, psychology and, more controversially, philosophy and theology. Recent advances in neuroscience are bringing us closer to a brain-based understanding of the NDE as an altered state of consciousness.

To fully embrace these findings we must leave behind the restrictive shackles of science and religio-political policy and embrace a new paradigm based heightened upon human spiritual experience. This will open our civilization to a dimension of mind in which the Oracle dwells and all can experience the Blue Lord.

SA

The returns us to *Sa*, the other half of the Saba word equation. *Sa*, the Egyptian word for the *wise* or *holy* (blue) *blood of Isis*. Like its counterpart the Hindu *soma* it made pharaohs wise and immortal.

211

Interestingly, *sa* is found in the Egyptian *sas*, the

Assyrian *sissa*, and Sanskrit *sas*, all meaning *six* .

As I discussed in *God Making*, the holy blood of Isis became the holy blood of Christ (*IS-SA* in India), which is actually a combination of blood and *holy water*, or what used to be called the *Lustral Water*.[21] This blood insures longevity, increases intelligence and enables us to demonstrate the advanced capabilities of the Oracle.

With the advancements in medical nanotechnology it could be a medical reality within the next two decades.

On the drawing board of nano wizards are much-hyped medical nanites that could patrol your body, and armed with knowledge of your DNA, repel any foreign invaders by forming an artificial immune system. The common cold would no longer exist, nor would threats of any biological or viral infection. Biological warfare would then cease to be a threat, also.

With medical nanites, we can not only extend our lives (by replacing our bodies), but also **stop completely** the aging process.

Of utmost interest to us is the belief that this blood contained (or enabled access to) the Great Mother' Sophia

or the Pleroma's -- -- spirit of all sacred wisdom or intelligence which the Greeks called ***nous***. *Nous* is the root of the *Noosphere*, the name given to the holographic library of the Global Mind present at the 12 oracular centers by the French theologian Teilhard de Chardin.

The sacred knowledge, it seems, concerns the ship of

life itself . Supporting this notion is the fact that
the Greek for ship is *naus*, which may be equated with
nous, meaning the mind. As noted, *rig* or mast of the ship
may have received its name from the mast of the ship of
knowledge (the Rig Veda).

The Oracle, among other things, possesses knowledge
of how to turn water into wine (in their blood) in order to
connect with the knowledge in the *Noosphere* and
download the knowledge that makes one an Oracle. The
rod or *ray* of life in Jesus' hand symbolized this knowledge
(that detail will be explored momentarily). Putting on this

'fleece' enabled the opening of the and connecting

with the Self or Source of Creation.

These traditions were evidently of particular interest to
Salvador Dali (1904–1989) who hung a dodecahedron
behind Jesus at the Last Supper (1955). This extraordinary
painting is one in a series of controversial paintings by Dali
with evocative Gnostic Christian meets hyperspace physics
themes. It hangs in the National Gallery of Art in
Washington D.C., despite efforts of various directors to
have it removed and steal it away to an obscure corner in a
basement.[22]

213

The Last Supper (1955), *Salvador Dali. Natonal Gallery of Art. Washington, D.C.*

In my opinion Dali's *The Last Supper* is an alchemical statement related to the mysteries of the 12-angled True Earth and provides a key to interpreting the 12 gates of the New Jerusalem. It portrays the Oracle revealing his secret.

Dali stated that this painting was an "arithmetic and philosophical cosmogony based on the paranoiac sublimity of the number twelve...the pentagon contains microcosmic man: Christ". The painting is rendered in such a way that one may think the message is Jesus pointing his finger. He sits in a commanding posture at the center of the pentagon and with a radiant glare, suggesting knowledge. He is the Oracle. There is a saying that when one points to the moon, the finger is not the moon. Don't mistake the finger for the moon. Jesus points his finger at the dodecahedron. Dali is directing us to the secret of the Oracle. He is also saying don't mistake Jesus for the secret. He is pointing to the secret. Those who engage Jesus in a slave-master relationship have confused the finger with the secret. The finger is not the secret. The dodecahedron is, but we've got to have some one to point us to it. This, modern science has done for us. The Oracle transcends the one who pointed the finger and becomes the finger pointer himself.

In the last chapter we will begin by considering a few more key examples of dodecahedral symbolism and conclude with a revelation of the Big Arcane Secret of the Oracle.

ORACLE OF THE ILLUMINATI

12.
THE BIG SECRET

According to Michael S. Schneider, the Founding Fathers of America -- Bacon's New Atlantis -- encoded the twelve-fold structure-function-order in many different ways. In *A Beginner's Guide To Constructing The Universe,*[1] Schneider explains the 12-fold canon of the Great Seal of the United States, America's corporate logo. Above the head a bald eagle is a glory of light and clouds enclosing pentagonal stars explicitly displaying the pattern. When he magnifies the glory's geometry and applies it to the whole of the seal, the underlying 12-fold plan upon which the seal was composed is revealed.

Another example of dodecahedral symbolism to be considered is that of 20th century occult scholar Rudolph Steiner, the man whom Adolf Hitler feared the most of all men.

On the evening of September 20, 1913, Dr. Steiner laid a foundation Stone (made of copper) into the hill at Dornach to celebrate the dedication of the completion of his spiritual center the Goetheanum. The holy stone was in the shape of a double pentagonal *dodecahedron* which he said "represents *the striving human soul* immersed as macrocosm in the microcosm." As opposed to the cuboctahedron, which represents a group of spiritual impulses, the similar 12-fold dodecahedron, represents "the cosmic image of the human soul." This building burned to the ground on New Years Eve, 1922 and remarkably, the original foundation Stone survived. One year later, at Christmas 1923, Dr. Steiner rededicated the Anthroposophical Society and the new Goetheanum.[2]

Steiner knew that the human body is the most significant spiritual symbol of all. In order comprehend the mysteries of this symbol and to sit at the dodecahedral round table with 12 holes we must develop our consciousess of the Blue Pearl. It is this consciousness that prepares the way for the Oracle to climb the ladder from Heaven to greet us. This is done in steps, observes Joseph Campbell. First, the initiate raises the god within as a child from the crib (*to steal* or *to lift* in its verb tense), as did Mary with Jesus and Maya with Buddha. At this level the inititiate engages in God Making, bringing the child/god to life within its own heart. This is called the "tiny dancer" within, set into motion by the song  of God.

Jesus points his finger at the 'round table' with 12 holes. A seat is held open for the prophesied coming of the 'Perfect Knight' who would achieve the Grail.

The next step in the development of the initiate is that of husband and wife. This is when the student, having raised or lifted the god-child or the divinity within and stolen the , begins the quest for the bride or spouse of God, Sophia. This is the level of the nun, the bride of

Christ. Nun is the name given to Joshua (Jesus) who stole the Blue Apples from the gods. *Nun*, we have seen, is the Egyptian name for the cosmic ocean, the waters of life or Nun or the Great Fish. The fifth level is that of love beyond love, or hyper-love, the next highest form of love. This is the love of the Oracle, who acts out of this knowledge.

Angel wearing a halo with 12 holes.

It is possible that the Greeks and the Gnostics inherited the ideas of the twelve-fold pattern from the Egyptians, who separated the Duat or Underworld into 12 divisions, variously and appropriately, described as *fields* or *plains* (a pun on planes), caverns or *halls*.

The Egyptian journey of the Pharaoh-initiate through the Duat (sometimes *Tuat*), as recounted by Zecharia Sitchin,[4] has several points of correspondence with Thomas's journey in *The Hymn of the Pearl*. In his journey to the Ladder to Heaven the Pharaoh encounters the Hidden

Place called the *Amen-Ta*, a domain described as a fortified circle. Amen-ta is also identified with *Ros-tau*, the place where the deceased king would collect the *efflux of Osiris*, the *fifth essence* ☥ that was required for his journey back to Heaven.[5]

Interestingly, Giza, like Amenta, is associated with Ros-tau (the mirror image *Stau-Ros*, the Greek term for the pillar of crucifixion). According to Utterance 553 of the Pyramid Texts, it was the 'efflux which issued from the putrefaction of Osiris'. Spell 1080 of the Coffin Texts tells exactly how this 'efflux' was brought to Earth.

'This is a sealed thing which is in darkness, with fire about it, which contains the efflux of Osiris, and it is put in Rostau (Giza, the Pillar of Crucifixion). It has been hidden since it fell from him (Osiris), and it is *what came down from him* on to the desert of sand'.

This is a tip-off that the Cosmic G-Spot Stimulator and the production of the *dew* or manna is being described. As Andrew Collins notes in *The Gods of Eden,* a circular chamber of the First Creation divided into twelve parts may be situated beneath the Giza plateau. He likens ito to the underground particle accelerator at CERN in Geneva.[6]

When the Pharaoh arrives at the Duat (Dew-at) he is only beginning his journey. He tunnels his way through the various 12 'hours' or halls of the Duat where he encounters numerous gods who all play a role in "opening the ways" for the Pharaoh. He sees the *Ben Ben*, the ship of the gods. All of his experiences are geared toward helping him attain the power to emerge from the Duat.

As if he is on some form of psychadelic trip, in the eleventh hour the Pharaoh meets the "Star Lady" and "Star Lord" whose attendant gods and goddesses are charged with equipping the Pharaoh for his upcoming "trip over the sky." In the company of some gods the Pharaoh enters a "Serpent" inside which he is to "shed the skin" and emerge "in the form of a rejuvenated Ra." Having entered the Serpent as a man, he emerges as a Falcon (a bird or bard), "equipped as a god." The Pharaoh now "lays down on the ground the *Mshdt*-garment"; he puts on his back the "Mark-garment"; he "takes his divine *Shuh*-vestment" (the Cloak of Light or Robe of Glory?) and he puts on the "collar of beloved Horus" which is like "a collar on the neck of Ra" (and the Blue Stones at the neck of Mari). Fully attired "the king has established himself there as a god, like them." He's good to go. Ready to launch. And he says so to the god beside him: "If thou goest to Heaven so will the king go to Heaven."

The king is next led through a hidden door that opens to a tunnel called "Dawn at the End". The tunnel opens to a vestibule decorated with the Winged Disk emblem. He is given new instructions by the goddesses present who "shed light upon the road of Ra." A scepter representing Seth, the watcher leaves the Pharaoh awestruck.

The gods explain:

This cavern is the broad hall of Osiris
Wherein the wind is brought;
The north wind, refreshing,
Will raise thee, O king, as Osiris.

This was the spot from whence the Egyptian savior, Osiris, rose into the heavens.

The king is at the place of the Stairway to Heaven where he sees an object called "The Ascender to the Sky." Illustrations in the Book of the Dead (next page) portray the Divine Ladder as a high tower with the *Ankh* ('life') sign mounted to it. Two 'cherubim' tend the device, clueing us in that the Pillar of Osiris is being described. Levitating just above the outstretched arms of the Ascender is the Celestial

Disk, the pearl ◯ or hole of Heaven. This is the Stairway.

The Great Ascender or the Cosmic G-Spot Stimulator.

Guarded by a heron, the Stairway sits atop the ship of the Gods, a two-headed serpent boat. In the 12th hour of the Duat texts the Door to Heaven opens, the king riding his serpent ascends triumphantly beyond the orbit of the 12-angled Earth into the stars. His destination is the ATON, the disk of the Milky Way, specifically the star Field of the Blessed or nursery at its center.

Heron guarding the M arches (that resemble McDonald's golden arches) and the Stairway upon the Serpent Ship. The M's, I believe, correspond with the Cathar yoke symbol

. They signify the heron as the deliverer of the

tie or serpent rope   that binds or connects us to Heaven.

The serpent-ship with Stairway to Heaven in the Elysian Fields, From the Papyrus of Ani, The British Museum.

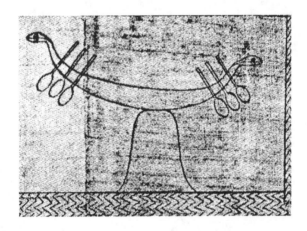

The serpent-ship resting upon the Primordial Mound in the Elysian Fields. From the Greenfield Papyrus, in the British Museum.

The serpent ship has morphed into a bearded human head on each side of the ship. The feather is the symbol for SHU, *"light, empty space."*

In Sumerian and Akkadin art this sequence of illustrations is uncannily reproduced. Enki is so closely connected with this serpent boat of Heaven that he is even depicted as a serpent-ship (as shown here).

In the Akkadian seal from the Oriental Museum at the University of Chicago on the previous page the Sun-god, Shemash, identified by his saw and the rays emanating from his shoulders, is depicted being transported in his serpent-boat. The prow of the boat ends in the figure of a bearded god, Enki, holding a forked punt-pole.

Enki ('the Serpent-man of Eden') delivers the secrets of salvation to Utnapushtim, the Sumerian Noah.

Priests of Enki tend a pillar of light shaped like the Egyptian Primordial Mound above which levitates a ring carrying gods. Note the Pillar mounted to a dragon-ship in the lower left background. British Museum.

A pillar, possibly the Cosmic G-Spot Stimulator, with 'apples' growing from it rests upon a dragon 'ship'. Two figures (herons, or bards of light) flank the pillar like the cherubim in the example of the Great Ascender on page 218.

In the two illustrations of the Elysian Fields we noted that the serpent ship (the 'wormhole'?), *in the form of a double-headed serpent*, rests upon the world mountain or Primeval Hill, presented in the first instance as a supporting stand or pillar and in the second as a column of water with a door ◯ in it. Featured on this ship is the Stairway to Heaven ⌐⌐ (*the Scala Dei*), the mythological flight of steps △▱, the Mayan ▛▜. The connection between the ship and the Stairway is made in the Egyptian word *khet*, which means "steps" and also "ship's mast". The mast of the ship is the Stairway to Heaven, because the ship itself is the conduit between Earth and Heaven.

It would be impossible to conclude this book without first noting that Johannes Kepler (1571–1630) placed a dodecahedron between Mars and Jupiter in his ingenious model of the solar system. Curiously, this is the location of the asteroid belt, which may be the debris field from the exploded planet called Tiamat or *Mare*.

Called the Watery Dragon of Chaos or the Great Mother Goddess of Wisdom, depending upon the story, she was a great ship that suffered an Atlantis-like, or Yaldabaoth-like fate, sinking into the dark waters of the night. A thousand things could have doomed Tiamat. Sumerian myth says it was the satellites of the jealous marauding planet called the Nibiru that split Tiamat in half. One half of Tiamat became the asteroid belt. The other half reformed into Earth.

The editors of the monumental *Chicago Assyrian Dictionary* have located and compiled all the places where the word "nibiru" and related forms of that word occur in Sumerian tablets. Nibiru has an assortment of meanings, all connected to the core idea of *"crossing"* or being some sort of *"crossing marker"* or *"crossing point"*.

The "root idea" of the *nibiru* word group and its forms almost always means something like "crossing" or "gate."

"Let *Nibiru* be the holder of the *crossing place of heaven and earth*," says one text. In the Gilgamesh epic, for example, we read the line (later reprised by Jesus in the beatitudes in the Sermon on the Mount): "Straight is the crossing point (the *nibiru*; a gateway), and narrow is the way that leads to it."

"Ferry, ford"; "ferry boat"; "(act of) ferrying" are also definitions of Nibiru.

When the accumulated meanings of Nibiru are tabulated we may interpret this word as referring to a "star, gate, crossing point" that enables one to Yalda-baoth *"pass through to her"* (Sophia, the Pleroma).

Nibiru is the Bridging Plane(t), connecting the material, mortal side of humanity with our higher spiritual immortal nature. On the other side of this bridge is wondrous Garden of Eden or Field of the Blessed, the hundreds of billions of galaxies, similar to our own, that comprise the known universe.

In this light Tiamat's planetary matter represents fragments of a mystery of the shattered Feminine Wisdom, of Sophia. Her story, examined in detail in my book *Ark of the Christos*, is the Atlantis story in the stars. Enki came to Earth on a rescue mission immediately after this cataclysm.

In Gnostic Christian myth Sophia (Tiamat) sent Christ to Earth in the form of a dove, the symbol of Tiamat and of the Oracle, to enter into Jesus at his baptism to rescue the souls...from the doomsday cataclysm of Tiamat/Atlantis, the Great Mother goddess who had descended into matter (in the form of Yaldabaoth). Jesus was considered the incarnation of Gnosis or knowledge.

Myth says that before her sinking Tiamat placed the Tablets of Creation on the Moon. These tablets were later brought to Earth by Enki who used them in the creation of the human body. As we have seen, these Stones correspond with the Blue Stones or Divine Particles of Sophia.

ORACLE OF THE ILLUMINATI

According to Madame H.P. Blavatsky, who reintroduced Eastern esotericism to the western mind at the beginning of the 20th century, the five-pointed star emblem of the Perfect Man, the Oracle, had been 'emblematically transformed into a crocodile', which was sometimes called the *Makara* (a pun on *Maker*), and was shown as a *serpent* **MV**.[7] Here, we are assured, we are on to one of the deepest secrets of arcane symbolism.

To reveal this Big Arcane Secret requires that we answer the question: Why does the pentagrammal *Perfect Man* or Oracle symbol transform into a *crocodile* or Ser-Pent? Does this relate to the Labyrinth at Crocodopolis in the Gnostic *Hymn of the Pearl*?

One answer comes from the Egyptian term for crocodile, *messias*, which is the root for the Hebrew term messiah, 'the perfect man'. As Laurence Gardner point out, it is from the words *Messeh* that the Hebrew stem MSSH derived. When vowels are added to this stem it forms the verb *mashiach* (to anoint) and the noun (*Messiah*), which means 'Anointed One' – i.e. the Christ, Christos, Messiah who comes from the Maker (*'Makara'*).[8] Jesus achieved this status only after being anointed by Mari Magdalene, the 'woman who knew the All' and the anointing oil ('all' in a Tennessee accent.)

The Maya also had the concept of the Axis Mundi, or World Tree, but in addition, they had a Crocodile Tree representing our galaxy -- the Milky Way, and they visited Hunab Ku -- the galactic center, which lies in the mouth of the crocodile (or dark rift as we call it).

It is no big secret that the Perfect Man becomes so by being anointed ('baptized') in the wisdom of Sophia. Surely, this is not the Big Arcane Secret of Blavatsky.

In my opinion, the Big Arcane Secret of the Makara (as well as of Tiamat and and Yaldabaoth) is that it was considered a bridge to other realms. MAKARA is the *'Ford Maker'* or 'Bridge Builder' of Indian tradition. This is exactly how the Sumerians defined Nibiru.

Blavatsky states that Makara (Nibiru) is the Gnostic Chozzar, another name for Chnoubis who *converts the sphere into a dodecagonal pyramid.*[9]

Makara ('maker') was portrayed as a sea monster that was an intermediary between Earth and Heaven. In the

Indian depiction shown here the Makara bears the or Word symbol on its cheek. He is easily identified with

Yaldabaoth and with Canah  .

Makara.

The canah-serpent (as well as the Promised Land of Canaan) is a symbol for a *con-duit*, defined by *Webster's* as 'a narrow passage, usually underground, for the purpose of *secret communication*... a *canal*, pipe, or passageway for the conveyance of fluids'. As we have seen, *Con* or *kon* means serpent (as we have seen in the word *Canah*, Mayan for great serpent). This is why a ring ◯ , especially the

con-centric circle ◎ , symbolizes the serpent and also the gate.

From this I conclude that the Big Arcane Secret is the method of transforming our consciousness to that of the Oracle and comprehending the secrets of the Ship of Life

. The oil, I believe, is a secretion from the pineal gland that ignites the 12 cranial nerves.

These secretions make us aware that we are all

holographic fragments of the Source,   , and prepare our consciousness for At-one-ment with the Ship.

I have presented several Sumerian cylinder seals depicting gods appearing between two mountains or a gate. In the final example, from Zecharia Sitchin's *The Stairway to* Heaven, I show a god, probably Shemash, appearing between the M with what I would interpret as the Cosmic G-Spot Stimulator behind him.

This scene could easily represent Thomas the Twin's return to the Pleroma. We can now appreciate that there is a serpent ship or wormhole behind the scenes of this image. Dazzling new information about this serpent ship may be forthcoming. Mayan prophecy, decoded by researcher John Major Jenkins,[10] and explored in detail in my book *Cloak of the Illuminati*, tells us that in 2012 a 'serpent rope' is going to emerge from the center of our Milky Way galaxy out of which will step a god of enlightenment, named Quetzalcoatl, the King of Tula. This is a modern rendition of the ancient Egyptian myth. In the context of this work it represents the arrival of the Oracle of the Illuminati.

NOTES AND REFERENCES

CHAPTER ONE: FROM CLOAK TO ORACLE

1. William Henry, *Cloak of the Illuminati* (Nashville, Scala Dei, 2002).
2. Mihail C. Roco and William Sims Bainbridge, Editors, *Converging Technologies for Improving Human Performance* (Prepublication on-line version, wtec.org/ConvergingTechnologies/Report/NBIC-pre-publication.pdf 2002), p. 63.
3. Genesis 6:4.
4. Dueteronomy 2:21-20; 9:2.
5. Numbers 13.
6. G.R.S. Mead, *Gnostic John the Baptizer* (Kila, MT, Kessinger Publishing), p. 42.
7. Zecharia Sitchin, *The Twelfth Planet* (New York, Avon, 1976).
8. Genesis 11:9.
9. II Kings 2:11
10. II Kings 2:13-16.
11. *Webster's Dictionary of the English Language* (New York, Publishers International Press, 1972), p. 906.
12. Ibid., *Twelfth Planet*, p. 130.
13. www.reference-guides.com
14. J.G.R. Forlong, *Rivers of Life: Sources and Streams of the Faiths of Man in All Lands* (Kila, MT, Kessinger Publishing), v. 1, p. 296-319.
15. Ibid., p. 130-131.
16. E.A. Wallis Budge, *The Gods of the Egyptians* (New York, Dover, 1969).

17. Father John Rossner, Ph.D., *In Search of the Primordial Tradition and The Cosmic Christ* (St. Paul, MN, Llewelyn, 1989), p. 163-171.
18. E. Valentia Straiton, *Celestial Ship of the North* (Kila, MT, Kessinger), p. 101.
19. www.nanotech-now.com/utility-fog.htm

CHAPTER TWO: THE RETURN OF SOPHIA

1. James M. Robinson, *The Nag Hammadi Library* (San Francisco, HaperSanFrancisco, 1988), p. 22-26.
2. www.wisdomworld.org/setting/thegnostics.html.
3. http://www.mapinc.org/drugnews/v03.n020.a08.html
4. www.livius.org/apark/apollonius/apollonius08.html#Divine men.
5. Translated by Marvin Meyer, *The Gospel of Thomas* (San Francisco, HarperSanFrancisco, 1992), p. 39.
6. J.G.R. Forlong, *Rivers of Life: Sources and Streams of the Faiths of Man in All Lands* (Kila, MT, Kessinger Publishing), v. 2, p. 296.
7. Harold Bayley, *The Lost Language of Symbolism* (New York, Carol Publishing Group, 1993), v. 1, p. 121.
8. Jean Chevalier and Alain Gheerbrant, *The Penguin Dictionary of Symbols* (New York, Penguin Books, 1969), p. 476.
9. Ibid., p. 902.
10. Kenneth Rayner Johnson, *The Fulcanelli Phenomenon* (Jersey, Channel Islands, Neville Spearman, 1980), p. 263.
11. Carl G. Liungman, *Dictionary of Symbols* (Santa Barbara, CA, ABC-CLIO, 1991), p. 278.
12. Ibid., *Rivers,* v. 1., p. 300.
13. E. Valentia Straiton, *Celestial Ship of the North* (Kila, MT, Kessinger), p. 70.

14. Ibid., *Lost Language*, v. 2, p. 258.
15. Harold Bayley, *A New Light On The Renaissance* (London, J.M. Dent), p. 104.
16. Ibid., *Dictionary of Symbols*, p. 168.
17. Ibid., p. 169.
18. Ibid., p. 169.
19. Ibid., p. 169.
20. Hunbatz Men, *Secrets of Mayan Science/Religion* (Santa Fe, NM, Bear & Co., 1990), p. 51.
21. Marija Gimbutas, *The Goddess and Gods of Old Europe* (Los Angeles, University of California Press, 1982), p. 101-102.
22. Ibid., p. 102.
23. Barbara G. Walker, *The Woman's Encyclopedia of Myths and Secrets* (New York, HarperCollins, 1983), p. 741.
24. Ibid., *Lost Language*, v. 2, p. 70.
25. Albert Churchward, *Signs & Symbols of Primordial Man* (Brooklyn, NY, A&B Publishers Group, 1993), p. 464.
26. www.sacred-texts.com/eso/oracle.htm
27. Ibid.
28. Ibid., *Rivers*, v. 1., p. 328.

CHAPTER THREE: THE COSMIC G-SPOT STIMULATOR

1. Barbara G. Walker, *The Woman's Encyclopedia of Myths and Secrets* (New York, HarperCollins, 1983), p. 7.
2. Godfrey Higgins, *The Anacalypsis* (Kila, MT, Kessinger Publishing), v. 1, p. 180.
3. Manly P. Hall, *The Secret Teachings of All the Ages* (Los Angeles, Philosophical Research Society, 1988), p. XXVI-XXVII.

4. *The New Strong's Concise Concordance* (Nashville, TN, Thomas Nelson, 1999), p. 254-255.
5. Ibid., p. 255.
6. Gordon Strachan, *Jesus the Master Builder: Druid Mysteries and the Dawn of Christianity* (Trowbridge, Wilts, Cromwell Press, 1998).
7. *Gospel of Thomas*, Sayings 12 and 13.
8. *Gospel of Thomas*, Saying 77.
9. Helmut Koester, "Introduction to The Gospel of Thomas", in James M. Robinson, *The Nag Hammadi Library* (San Francisco, HaperSanFrancisco, 1988), 124.
10. Stephan A. Hoeller, The Gnostic Jung (Wheaton, Ill., Quest Books, 1982), p.11.

CHAPTER FOUR: THE REALITY OF THE RULERS

1. James M. Robinson, *The Nag Hammadi Library* (San Francisco, HaperSanFrancisco, 1988), p. 161.
2. Ibid., p. 104.
3. Ibid., p. 170.
4. Harold Bayley, *The Lost Language of Symbolism* (New York, Carol Publishing Group, 1993), v. 2, p. 29.
5. Revelation 21:11.
6. E. Valentia Straiton, *Celestial Ship of the North* (Kila, MT, Kessinger), p. 101.
7. William Henry, *Ark of the Christos* (Nashville, TN, Scala Dei,2002).
8. Ibid., *Lost Language*, v. 2, p. 298.
9. Ibid.
10. Jeremy Narby, *The Cosmic Serpent* (New York, Jeremy Tarcher, 1998), p. 92.
11. Ibid.
12. members.aol.com/oldenwilde/members/diu/quadriv.html

13. R.A. Schwaller de Lubicz, *Symbol and Symbolic: Egypt, Science and the Evolution of Consciousness* (Brookline, MA, Autumn Press, 1978), p. 32.
14. Hunbatz Men, *The Secrets of Mayan Science/Religion* (Santa Fe, NM, Bear & Company, 1990), p. 119-129.
15. Ibid., p. 128.
16. Ibid., *Cosmic Serpent*, p. 93.
17. Ibid., *Lost Language*, v. 2, p. 299.
18. Michio Kaku, *Hyperspace: A Scientific Odyssey Through Parallel Universes, Time Warps and The Tenth Dimension* (New York, Oxford, 1994), p. 276-280.
19. Rene Guenon, *Fundamental Symbols: The Universal Language of Sacred Science* (Oxford, Quinta Essentia, 1962), p. 69.
20. Godfrey Higgins, *Anacalypsis* (Montana, USA, Kessinger Publishing) v.2, p. 5.
21. Barbara G. Walker, *The Woman's Encyclopedia of Myths and Secrets* (New York, HarperCollins, 1983), p. 584.
22. Musaios, *The Lion Path: You Can Take It With You* (Sardis, B.C., Horus House, 1990).
23. Ibid., p. 67.

CHAPTER FIVE: THE HYMN OF THE PEARL

1. Bentley Layton, *The Gnostic Scriptures* (New York, Doubleday, 1987), p. 366.
2. Zecharia Sitchin, *The Twelfth Planet* (New York, Avon Books, 1976), p. 124.
3. Ibid., *Gnostic Scriptures*, p. 366.
4. Ibid., p. 366.
5. Ibid., p. 372.
6. Ibid., p. 373.
7. www.buddhistdoor.com/resources/sutras/net_sutra.htm

8. Swami Muktananda, Secret of the Siddhas (South Fallsburg, NY, SYDA Foundation, 1980), p. 23.
9. Ibid., p. 22.
10. Ibid., p. 22.
11. www.people.virginia.edu/~rjh9u/blkysc82.html
12. Harold Bayley, The Lost Language of Symbolism (New York, Carol Publishing Group, 1993), v. 2, p. 79.
13. Webster's Dictionary of the English Language (New York, Publishers International Press, 1972), p. 775.
14. Jordan Maxwell, Priesthood of Illes.
15. James M. Robinson, The Nag Hammadi Library (San Francisco, HaperSanFrancisco, 1988), p. 173.
16. Ibid., Lost Language, v. 1, p. 221.
17. Father John Rossner, Ph.D., In Search of the Primordial Tradition and The Cosmic Christ (St. Paul, MN, Llewelyn, 1989), p. 149.
18. Ibid., p. 144.
19. Ibid., p. 150.
20. Laurence Gardner, Lost Secrets of the Sacred Ark (London, Element, 2003).
21. Graham Hancock, The Sign and the Seal (New York, Crown Publishing, 1992), p. 67-69.
22. Robert Graves, The White Goddess (New York, The Noonday Press, 1948), p. 269.
23. Ezekiel 28:13, 1:26, 10:1.
24. J.G.R. Forlong, Rivers of Life: Sources and Streams of the Faiths of Man in All Lands (Kila, MT, Kessinger Publishing), v. 1, p. 383.
25. 1 Kings 21:1.
26. Jean Chevalier and Alain Gheerbrant, The Dictionary of Symbols (New York, Penguin Books, 1969), p. 1067.
27. Matthew 13:45-46.
28. Matthew 13:44.

29. Ibid., *Nag Hammadi Library*, p. 287.

30. www.touregypt.net/featurestories/lotus.htm.

31. Barbara G. Walker, *The Woman's Encyclopedia of Myths and Secrets* (New York,HarperCollins, 1983), p. 542.

32. Ibid. p. 542.

33. Ibid. p. 543.

34. Ibid. p. 543.

CHAPTER SIX: REALM OF THE ILLUMINATI

We will explore more of his concepts of the Pleroma momentarily. For the moment, it is important to note that Jung had two points of convergence with the ideas we have explored. First, according to biographer Richard Noll in The Aryan Christ: The Secret Life of Carl Jung, Jung claimed he became the lion-headed god in a visionary ecstasy in December 1913. Second, on page six of his book Word and Image, edited by Aniela Jaffe, is a copy of the Jung family crest. The caption reads: "The crest originally bore a phoenix, or according to another version, a butterfly crawling out of its cocoon. Both emblems would suggest the idea of youth (jung = "young"). C.G. Jung's grandfather altered the crest. A BLUE CROSS and a BLUE CLUSTER OF GRAPES symbolized the heavenly and the terrestrial spirit, and the unifying symbol is the star, which evokes the alchemists' gold." (All caps mine.)

1. Richard Noll, *The Aryan Christ* (New York, Random House, 1997)
2. Gospel of Thomas, Saying 22.
3. **www.khaldea.com/rudhyar/toohuman.shtm**.
4. Zecharia Sitchin, *The Twelfth Planet* (New York, Avon Books, 1976), p. 336-361.
5. Ibid., p. 133-134.
6. David Ovason, *The Secret Architecture of Our Nation's Capital* (New York, HarperCollins, 1999), p. 183.

7. Ibid., p. 183.
8. Harold Bayley, *The Lost Language of Symbolism* (New York, Carol Publishing Group, 1993), v. 1, p. 200.
9. Ibid., *Lost Language*, v. 1, p. 354.

CHAPTER SEVEN: FRANCIS BACON: ORACLE

1. The Gospel of the Infancy 19:17-19.
2. Harold Bayley, *The Lost Language of Symbolism* (New York, Carol Publishing Group, 1993), v. 2, p. 12.
3. Manly P. Hall, *The Secret Teachings of All the Ages* (Los Angeles, Philosophical Research Society, 1988), p. CLXVII.
4. Sirbacon.org/links/whitneyemblem.html
5. Ibid., p. CLXVII.
6. Ibid., p. CLXVII.
7. Ibid., p. XLXVIII.
8. Ibid., p. XLXVII.
9. www.sirbacon.org/leith.htm.
10. Kenneth Mackenzie, *The Royal Masonic Cyclopaedia* (Great Britain, The Aquarian Press, 1987), p. 386-387.
11. Keith Laidler, *The Head of God: The Lost Treasure of the Templars* (Great Britain, Weidenfeld & Nicolson, 1998), p. 164-185.
12. Dr. Hugh Schonfield, *The Essene Odyssey* (London, Element, 1984), p. 164.
13. www.templarhistory.com/shah.html
14. Lynn Picknett & Clive Prince, *The Templar Revelation: Secret Guardians of the True Identity of Christ* (London, Bantam Press, 1997), p. 110.
15. Barbara G. Walker, *The Woman's Encyclopedia of Myths and Secrets* (New York, HarperCollins, 1983), p. 854.
16. Ibid., p. 657.

17. Hany Assaad & Daniel Kolos, *Hieroglyphic Inscriptions of the Treasures of Tutankhamun Translated* (Ontario, Benben Publications, 1979), p. 122.
18. Ibid., p. 129.
19. Matthew 26:28, Mark 14:24, Luke 22:20.
20. *The New Strong's Concise Concordance* (Nashville, TN, Thomas Nelson, 1999), p. 340.
21. Hugh Schonfield, *The Essene Odyssey: The Mystery of the True Teacher and the Essene Impact on the Shaping of Human Destiny* (Shaftesbury, Dorset, Element, 1984), p. 164.

CHAPTER EIGHT: ABYDOS AND THE HEAD OF GOD

1. E.A. Wallis Budge, *Osiris and the Egyptian Resurrection* (New York, Dover, 1973), v. 1, p. 289.
2. Omm Sety and Hanny El Zeini, *Abydos: Holy City of Ancient Egypt* (Los Angeles, CA, LL Company, 1981).
3. Lucy Lamy, *Egyptian Mysteries: New Light on Ancient Knowledge* (New York, Thames & Hudson, 1981), p. 17.
4. Alan Alford, *The Phoenix Solution: Secrets of a Lost Civilization* (London, Hodder and Stoughton, 1998), p. 257.
5. Andrew Collins, *Gods of Eden* (London, Headline, 1998), p. 173.
6. Ibid., *Woman's Encyclopedia*, p. 944.
7. Ibid., p. 944.
8. Harold Bayley, *The Lost Language of Symbolism* (New York, Carol Publishing Group, 1993), v.2, p. 18.
9. Ahmed Osman, *The House of the Messiah* (London, Grafton, 1993).
10. 1 Peter 2:6.
11. Ephesians 3:15.

12. Isaiah 65:8.
13. 1 Corinthians 12:12-27.
14. Jean Houston, *Godseed: The Journey of Christ* (Wheaton, IL, Quest Books, 1992), p. 53.
15. Ibid., p. 53.
16. 1 Corinthians 1:25.
17. www.blastitude.com/13/ETERNITY/forward_of_eternity.htm
18. http://www.sacred-texts.com/the/iu/iu101.htm
19. Michael White, *Isaac Newton: The Last Sorcerer* (Reading, Mass, Addison-Wesley, 1997).

CHAPTER NINE: ENKI AND THE FLOWER OF LIGHT

1. Hany Assaad & Daniel Kolos, *Hieroglyphic Inscriptions of the Treasures of Tutankhamun Translated* (Ontario, Benben Publications, 1979), p. 122.
2. Ibid., p. 127.
3. Barbara G. Walker, *The Woman's Encyclopedia of Myths and Secrets* (New York, HarperCollins, 1983), p. 581.
4. www.sirbacon.org/links/chronos.html
5. Richard Hinckley Allen, *Star Names: Their Lore and Meaning* (New York, Dover, 1963), p. 433.
6. space.com/scienceastronomy/astronomy/newton_galaxy_010625.html
7. Revelation 19:16.
8. Revelation 19:12.
9. Revelation 19:13.
10. Flavia Anderson, *The Ancient Secret: Fire From the Sun* (Kent, R.I.L.K.O., 1987), p. 40.
11. Ibid., p. 40.
12. Jean Danielou, *Primitive Christian Symbols* (Baltimore, Helicon Press, 1963,) p. 89-95.

13. William Henry, *God Making* (Nashville, TN, Scala Dei, 2001).
14. G.R.S. Mead, *Gnostic John the Baptizer* (Kila, MT, Kessinger Publishing), p. 5.
15. www.yashanet.com/studies/judaism101/sidebars/ohr.htm
16. John Michell, *The Temple of Jerusalem: A Revelation* (York Beache, MN, Samuel Weiser, 2000), p. 9.
17. Ibid., p. 9.
18. Ibid., p. 10.
19. Ibid., p. 39.

CHAPTER TEN: THE GOD HEAD AND THE DODECAHEDRON

1. William Henry, *The A~tomic Christ: F.D.R.'s Search for the Secret Temple of the Christ Light* (Nashville, TN, Scala Dei, 2000).
2. www.coasttocoastam.com/shows/2003/11/02.html#lear
3. Col. Philip J. Corso, (Ret.), *The Day AfterRoswell* (New York, Pocket Books, 1997).
4. F. David Peat, *Superstrings and the Search for the Theory of Everything* (New York, Contemporary Books, 1988).
5. Dr. C.G. Jung, *Psychology and Alchemy* (Princeton, N.J, Princeton Univerity Press, 1968), p. 239.
6. F. David Peat, *Synchronicity: The Bridge Between Matter and Mind* (New York, Bantam Books, 1987), p. 65.
7. Ibid., p. 66.
8. Ibid., p. 196.
9. Tielhard de Chardin, *Christianity and Evolution* (New York, Harcourt, Brace, Jovanovich, 1974).
10. Ibid., p. 16.
11. Ibid., p. 17.
12. Ibid., p. 19.

13. Ibid., p. 67.
14. Ibid.., p. 68-69.
15. Laurence Gardner, *Lost Secrets of the Sacred Ark* (London, Element, 2003).
16. Genesis 28:12.
17. Genesis 28:17.
18. Genesis 49:1-28.
19. Exodus 28:30.
20. Exodus 28:1.
21. Exodus 18:2-3.
22. Exodus 28:4.
23. 1 Sam 23:6-12, 30:7-8.
24. See Exodus 28:30; Leviticus 8:8; Numbers 27:21; Deuteronomy 33:8; 1 Samuel 28:6; Ezra 2:63; Nehemiah 7:65.
25. http://www.edgarcayce.org/am/urimthummim.html.

CHAPTER ELEVEN: THE STAR WALKER

1. Andrew Collins, *Gods of Eden* (London, Headline, 1998), p. 207.
2. Robert Lawlor, *Sacred Geometry: Philosophy and Practice* (London, Thames and Hudson, 1982), p. 106.
3. E.A. Wallis Budge, *Egyptian Hieroglyphic Dictionary* (New York, Dover, 1920), v. 2, p. 655b.
4. Ibid.
5. Ibid.
6. Timothy Freke & Peter Gandy, *The Jesus Mysteries* (New York, Random House, 1999), p. 101.
7. Robert Temple, The Crystal Sun: Rediscovering a Lost Technology of the Ancient World (London, Century, 2000), p. 103.

8. Lucie Lamy, *Egyptian Mysteries: New Light on Ancient Knowledge* (New York, Thames & Hudson, 1981), p. 65.
9. Manly P. Hall, *The Secret Teachings of All the Ages* (Los Angeles, Philosophical Research Society, 1988), p. CXXLV.
10. Exodus 17:12.
11. Ibid., *Secret Teachings*, XV.
12. Itzhak Bentov, *Stalking the Wild Pendulum* (New York, Dutton, 1977), p. 82.
13. Ajit Mookerjee, *Kundalini: The Arousal of the Inner Energy* (Rochester, VT, Destiny Books, 1982).
14. Rick Strassman, M.D., *DMT: The Spirit Molecule* (Rochester, VT, Park Street Press, 2001), p. 56).
15. Ibid., p. 2041-208.
16. Ibid., p. 214.
17. John E. Mack, *Abduction* (New York, Ballantine, 1994) and *Passport to the Cosmos* (New York, Crown, 1999).
18. Ibid., DMT, p. 219.
19. leda.lycaeum.org/?ID=5271
20. http://www.ortho.lsumc.edu/Faculty/Marino/Papers/108 Piezoelectricity.pdf.
21. J.G.R. Forlong, *Rivers of Life: Sources and Streams of the Faiths of Man in All Lands* (Kila, MT, Kessinger Publishing), v. 2, p. 94.
22. Meredith Etherington-Smith, *The Persistence of Memory: A Biography of Salvador Dali* (New York, Random House, 1992), p. 339.
23.
24. George W. Carey & Inez E. Perry, *God-Man, The Word Made Flesh* (Kila, MT, Kessinger Publishing Co.), p. 71-72.
25. Ibid., p 71-72.
26. Ibid., p. 72.
27. Barbara G. Walker, *The Woman's Encyclopedia of Myths and Secrets* (New York,HarperCollins, 1983), p. 464.

28. Jean Chevalier and Alain Gheerbrant, *The Dictionary of Symbols* (New York, Penguin Books, 1969), p. 503.

CHAPTER TWELVE: THE BIG SECRET

1. Michael S. Schneider, *A Beginner's guide to Constructing the Universe* (New York, HarperCollins, 1994),p. 204-207.
2. John Fletcher, *Art Inspired by Rudolf Steiner* (Great Britain, Mercury Arts, 1987), p. 40-43.
3. Joseph Campbell, *The Eastern Way* (Minneapolis, MN, Highbridge), audio.
4. Zecharia Sitchin, *The Stairway to Heaven* (New York, Avon, 1980), p. 47-67.
5. Alan F. Alford, *When the Gods Came Down* (London, Hodder&Stoughton, 2000), p. 70.
6. Andrew Collins, *Gods of Eden* (London, Headline, 1998), p. 208-209.
7. H.P. Blavatsky, *The Secret Doctrine* (New York, Theosophical Publishing, 1888), v. 2, p. 576-577.
8. Laurence Gardner, *Genesis of the Grail Kings* (London, Bantam, 1999), p. 124.
9. Ibid., *Secret Doctrine*, p.v. 2, p. 577.
10. John Major Jenkins, *Maya Cosmogenesis 2012* (Santa Fe, NM, Bear & Co., 1998).

William Henry is an investigative mythologist. His primary expertise and mission is finding and interpreting ancient gateway stories which feature advanced technology for raising of spiritual vibration and increasing our body's innate healing ability.

He regularly appears on radio programs and lectures internationally. He has inspired a new generation of seekers with his interpretations of ancient mysteries, edgy science and the promise of the new millennium. He lives in Nashville, Tennessee.

Visit his website:

www.Williamhenry.net

FROM THE CLOAK OF THE ILLUMINATI TO THE STARGATES OF THE GODS

Available at: Williamhenry.net:

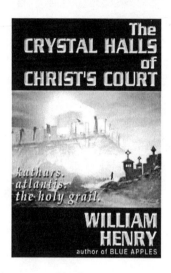

THE CRYSTAL HALLS OF CHRIST'S COURT
Kathars, Atlantis, The Holy Grail
Coil Bound
360 Pages, Fully Illustrated,
$24.95
"I have been studying the secrets of esoteric Christianity and Masonry for many years, and I have found what I believe to be one of the great masterworks of this field. In a stunning tour-de-force of intelligence and brilliant mythological detective work, William Henry has created the Crystal Halls of Christ's Court."
Whitley Strieber

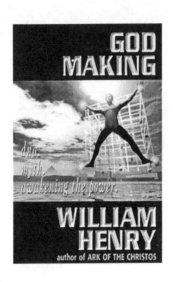

GOD MAKING
DNA, Myth, Awakening the Power
Coil Bound
278 pages. Fully illustrated.
$24.95

William has researched the medical myths of the ancients and has found striking similarity between these myths and the discoveries of modern scientific discoveries about DNA. In God Making, William reveals advanced ancient scientific knowledge about the Soul, the Self and the body (including DNA) encoded in myth and legend.

BLUE APPLES
Stargate Secrets of Jesus and Mary Magdalene
Coil Bound
252 Pages, Fully Illustrated
$24.95
The ancient stories assure us that stargates are real. They exist. And Jesus and Mary Magdalene may have opened one. Enter the phenomenal mystery of Rennes-le-Chateau, the remote village in Southern France where Mary Magdalene lived helived her last days. See amazing ancient depictions of the Holy Grail as a stargate technology.

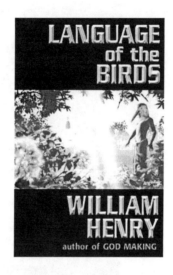

THE LANGUAGE OF THE BIRDS
Our Angelic Connection
Coil Bound
140 pages, Fully Illustrated.
$19.95

For centuries an idea has existed that there once was a language of the angels. This language, called the Language of the Birds, was spoken in the Garden of Eden, but was lost. William reveals the secrets of the Language of the Birds and our angelic connection.

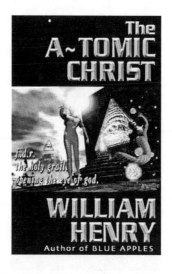

THE A~TOMIC CHRIST: FDR's SEARCH FOR THE SECRET TEMPLE OF THE CHRIST LIGHT
Coil Bound
325 pages fully illustrated
$24.95

The definitive work revealing the hidden history behind the 1934 Nicholas Roerich expedition to Mount Meru, Mongolia, commissioned by FDR to find the lost secrets of the Holy Grail. William Henry lays out the facts in what is easily one of the most under-reported stories of the 20th century.

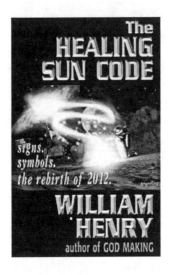

THE HEALING SUN CODE: SIGNS. SYMBOLS. THE REBIRTH OF 2012
Coil Bound
377 pages, Fully Illustrated
$24.95

Maya prophets claimed 2012 would be a moment of new creation resulting in the transformation of our world. To use a term, with which we are now familiar, our world will be 'born again'. The book examines the fascinating pictures of the Healing Sun Maya science and religion draws for us in more detail.

ARK OF THE CHRISTOS: THE MYTHOLOGY, SYMBOLISM AND PROPHECY OF THE RETURN OF PLANET X AND THE AGE OF TERROR
Coil Bound
377 pages, Fully Illustrated
$24.95

For the ancient Sumerians, the story of Planet X was the guiding myth of civilization. In this groundbreaking new guide William Henry provides keys to the esoteric knowledge hidden in the symbolism of the Shining Ones and our present Age of Terror.

Scala Dei Publishing
P.O. Box 2143
Hendersonville, TN 37075
www.williamhenry.net
Scala Dei
1-615-292-7863

ORACLE OF THE ILLUMINATI

CONSPIRACY & HISTORY

PIRATES & THE LOST TEMPLAR FLEET
The Secret Naval War Between the Templars & the Vatican
by David Hatcher Childress

Childress takes us into the fascinating world of maverick sea captains who were Knights Templar (and later Scottish Rite Free Masons) who battled the Vatican, and the Spanish and Italian ships that sailed for the Pope. The lost Templar fleet was originally based at La Rochelle in southern France, but fled to the deep fiords of Scotland upon the dissolution of the Order by King Phillip. This banned fleet of ships was later commanded by the St. Clair family of Rosslyn Chapel (birthplace of Free Masonry). St. Clair and his Templars made a voyage to Canada in the year 1298 AD, nearly 100 years before Columbus! Later, this fleet of ships and new ones to come, flew the Skull and Crossbones, the symbol of the Knights Templar. They preyed on the ships of the Vatican coming from the rich ports of the Americas and were ultimately known as the Pirates of the Caribbean. Chapters include: 10,000 Years of Seafaring; The Knights Templar & the Crusades; The Templars and the Assassins; The Lost Templar Fleet and the Jolly Roger; Maps of the Ancient Sea Kings; Pirates, Templars and the New World; Christopher Columbus—Secret Templar Pirate?; Later Day Pirates and the War with the Vatican; Pirate Utopias and the New Jerusalem; more.
320 PAGES. 6x9 ILLUSTRATED. BIBLIOGRAPHY. $16.95. CODE: PLTF

CLOAK OF THE ILLUMINATI
Secrets, Transformations, Crossing the Star Gate
by William Henry

Thousands of years ago the stargate technology of the gods was lost. Mayan Prophecy says it will return by 2012, along with our alignment with the center of our galaxy. In this book: Find examples of stargates and wormholes in the ancient world; Examine myths and scripture with hidden references to a stargate cloak worn by the Illuminati, including Mari, Nimrod, Elijah, and Jesus; See rare images of gods and goddesses wearing the Cloak of the illuminati; Learn about Saddam Hussein and the secret missing library of Jesus; Uncover the secret Roman-era eugenics experiments at the Temple of Hathor in Denderah, Egypt; Explore the duplicate of the Stargate Pillar of the Gods in the Illuminists' secret garden in Nashville; Discover the secrets of manna, the food of the angels, Jesus and the Illuminati; more. Chapters include: Seven Stars Under Three Stars; The Long Walk; Squaring the Circle; The Mill of the Host; The Miracle Garment; The Fig; Nimrod: The Mighty Man; Nebuchadnezzar's Gate; The New Mighty Man; more.
238 PAGES. 6x9 PAPERBACK. ILLUSTRATED. BIBLIOGRAPHY. INDEX. $16.95. CODE: COIL

GUARDIANS OF THE HOLY GRAIL
by Mark Amaru Pinkham

Although the Templar Knights had been schooled in the legend of Jesus Christ and his famous chalice while in their homeland of France, during their one hundred years in the Holy Land they discovered that Jesus's Holy Grail was but one of a long line of Holy Grail manifestations, and that a lineage of Guardians of the Holy Grail had existed in Asia for thousands of years prior to the birth of the Messiah. This book presents this extremely ancient Holy Grail lineage from Asia and how the Knights Templar were initiated into it. It also reveals how the ancient Asian wisdom regarding the Holy Grail became the foundation for the Holy Grail legends of the west while also serving as the bedrock of the European Secret Societies, which included the Freemasons, Rosicrucians, and the Illuminati. Also: The Fisher Kings; The Middle Eastern mystery schools, such as the Assassins and Yezidhi; The ancient Holy Grail lineage from Sri Lanka and the Templar Knights' initiation into it; The head of John the Baptist and its importance to the Templars; The secret Templar initiation with grotesque Baphomet, the infamous Head of Wisdom; more.
248 PAGES. 6x9 PAPERBACK. ILLUSTRATED. BIBLIOGRAPHY. $16.95. CODE: GOHG

RETURN OF THE SERPENTS OF WISDOM
by Mark Amaru Pinkham

According to ancient records, the patriarchs and founders of the early civilizations in Egypt, India, China, Peru, Mesopotamia, Britain, and the Americas were the Serpents of Wisdom—spiritual masters associated with the serpent—who arrived in these lands after abandoning their beloved homelands and crossing great seas. While bearing names denoting snake or dragon (such as Naga, Lung, Djedhi, Amaru, Quetzalcoatl, Adder, etc.), these Serpents of Wisdom oversaw the construction of magnificent civilizations within which they and their descendants served as the priest kings and as the enlightened heads of mystery school traditions. Pinkham recounts the history of these "Serpents"—where they came from, why they came, the secret wisdom they disseminated, and why they are returning now.
400 PAGES. 6x9 PAPERBACK. ILLUSTRATED. REFERENCES. $16.95. CODE: RSW

THE STONE PUZZLE OF ROSSLYN CHAPEL
by Philip Coppens

Rosslyn Chapel is revered by Freemasons as a vital part of their history, believed by some to hold evidence of pre-Columbian voyages to America, assumed by others to hold important relics, from the Holy Grail to the Head of Christ, the Scottish chapel is a place full of mystery. The history of the chapel, its relationship to freemasonry and the family behind the scenes, the Sinclairs, is brought to life, incorporating new, previously forgotten and heretofore unknown evidence. Significantly, the story is placed in the equally enigmatic landscape surrounding the chapel, which includes features from Templar commanderies to prehistoric markings, from an ancient kingly site to the South to Arthur's Seat directly north of the chapel. The true significance and meaning of the chapel is finally unveiled: it is a medieval stone book of esoteric knowledge "written" by the Sinclair family, one of the most powerful and wealthy families in Scotland, chosen patrons of Freemasonry.
124 PAGES. 6x9 PAPERBACK. ILLUSTRATED. $12.00. CODE: SPRC

THE HISTORY OF THE KNIGHTS TEMPLARS
by Charles G. Addison, introduction by David Hatcher Childress

Chapters on the origin of the Templars, their popularity in Europe and their rivalry with the Knights of St. John, later to be known as the Knights of Malta. Detailed information on the activities of the Templars in the Holy Land, and the 1312 AD suppression of the Templars in France and other countries, which culminated in the execution of Jacques de Molay and the continuation of the Knights Templars in England and Scotland; the formation of the society of Knights Templars in London; and the rebuilding of the Temple in 1816. Plus a lengthy intro about the lost Templar fleet and its North American sea routes.
395 PAGES. 6x9 PAPERBACK. ILLUSTRATED. $16.95. CODE: HKT

SAUNIER'S MODEL AND THE SECRET OF RENNES-LE-CHATEAU
The Priest's Final Legacy
by André Douzet

Berenger Saunière, the enigmatic priest of the French village of Rennes-le-Château, is rumored to have found the legendary treasure of the Cathars. But what became of it? In 1916, Saunière created his ultimate clue: he went to great expense to create a model of a region said to be the Calvary Mount, indicating the "Tomb of Jesus." But the region on the model does not resemble the region of Jerusalem. Did Saunière leave a clue as to the true location of his treasure? And what is that treasure? After years of research, André Douzet discovered this model—the only real clue Saunière left behind as to the nature and location of his treasure—and the possible tomb of Jesus.
116 PAGES. 6x9 PAPERBACK. ILLUSTRATED. BIBLIOGRAPHY. $12.00. CODE: SMOD

24 hour credit card orders—call: 815-253-6390 fax: 815-253-6300
email: auphq@frontiernet.net   www.adventuresunlimitedpress.com   www.wexclub.com

NEW BOOKS

THE WORLD CATACLYSM IN 2012
Maya Calendar Countdown
by Patrick Geryl

In his previous book, *The Orion Prophecy*, author Geryl theorized that the lost civilization of Atlantis was destroyed by a huge cataclysm engendered by changes in sunspot activity affecting Earth's magnetic poles and atmosphere. Having experienced earlier catastrophes, the Atlanteans had developed amazing astronomical and mathematical knowledge that enabled them to predict the date of their continent's demise. They devised a survival plan, and were able to pass along their knowledge to civilizations we know as the Maya and Old Egyptians. Here, Geryl shows that the mathematics and astronomy of the ancient Egyptians and Maya are related, and have similar predictive power which should be taken very seriously. He cracks their hidden codes that show definitively that the next earth-consuming cataclysm will occur in 2012, and calls urgently for the excavation of the Labyrinth of ancient Egypt, a storehouse of Atlantean knowledge which is linked in prophecy to the May predictions.

256 PAGES. 6x9 PAPERBACK. ILLUSTRATED. REFERENCES. $16.95. CODE: WC20

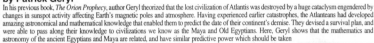

HIDDEN NATURE
The Startling Insights of Viktor Schauberger
by Alick Bartholomew, foreword by David Bellamy

Victor Schauberger (1885-1958) pioneered a new understanding of the Science of Nature, (re)discovering its primary laws and principles, unacknowledged by contemporary science. From studying the fast flowing streams of the unspoilt Alps, he gained insights into water as a living organism. He showed that water is like a magnetic tape; it can carry information that may either enhance or degrade the quality of organisms. Our failure to understand the need to protect the quality of water is the principle cause of environmental degradation on the planet. Schauberger warned of climatic chaos resulting from deforestation and called for work with free energy machines and energy generation. Chapters include: Schauberger's Vision; Different Kinds of Energy; Attraction & Repulsion of Opposites; Nature's Patterns & Shapes; Energy Production; Motion, Key to Balance; Atmosphere/Electricity; The Nature of Water; Hydrological Cycle; Formation of Springs; How Rivers Flow; Supplying Water; The Role of the Forests; Tree Metabolism; Soil Fertility and Cultivation; Organic Cultivation; The Energy Revolution; Harnessing Implosion Power; Viktor Schauberger & Society; more.

288 PAGES. 7x10 PAPERBACK. ILLUSTRATED. REFERENCES. INDEX. $22.95. CODE: HNAT

FROM LIGHT INTO DARKNESS
The Evolution of Religion in Ancient Egypt
by Stephen S. Mehler

Building on the esoteric information first revealed in Land of Osiris, this exciting book presents more of Abd'El Hakim's oral traditions, with radical new interpretations of how religion evolved in prehistoric and dynastic Khemit, or Egypt. * Have popular modern religions developed out of practices in ancient Egypt? * Did religion in Egypt represent only a shadow of the spiritual practices of prehistoric people? * Have the Western Mystery Schools such as the Rosicrucian Order evolved from these ancient systems? * Author Mehler explores the teachings of the King Akhenaten and the real Moses, the true identity of the Hyksos, and Akhenaten's connections to The Exodus, Judaism and the Rosicrucian Order. Here for the first time in the West, are the spiritual teachings of the ancient Khemitians, the foundation for the coming new cycle of consciousness—The Awakening; more.

240 PAGES. 6x9 PAPERBACK. ILLUSTRATED. REFERENCES. $16.95. CODE: FLID

ORACLE OF THE ILLUMINATI
Coincidence, Cocreation, Contact
By William Henry

Investigative mythologist William Henry follows up his best-selling Cloak of the Illuminati with this illustration-packed treatise on the secret codes, oracles and technology of ancient Illuminati. His primary expertise and mission is finding and interpreting ancient gateway stories which feature advanced technology for raising of spiritual vibration and increasing our body's innate healing ability. Chapters include: From Cloak to Oracle; The Return of Sophia; The Cosmic G-Spot Stimulator; The Reality of the Rulers; The Hymn of the Pearl; The Realm of the Illuminati; Francis Bacon: Oracle; Abydos and the Head of Sophia; Enki and the Flower of Light; The God Head and the Dodecahedron; The Star Walker; The Big Secret; more.

243 PAGES. 6x9 PAPERBACK. ILLUSTRATED. NOTES & REFERENCES. $16.95. CODE: ORIL

THE GIZA DEATH STAR DESTROYED
The Ancient War For Future Science
by Joseph P. Farrell

This is the third and final volume in the popular *Giza Death Star* series, physicist Farrell looks at what eventually happened to the 10,000-year-old Giza Death Star after it was deployed—it was destroyed by an internal explosion. Recapping his earlier books, Farrell moves on to events of the final days of the Giza Death Star and its awesome power. These final events, eventually leading up to the destruction of this giant machine, are dissected one by one, leading us to the eventual abandonment of the Giza Military Complex—an event that hurled civilization back into the Stone Age. Chapters include: The Mars-Earth Connection; The Lost "Root Races" and the Moral Reasons for the Flood; The Destruction of Krypton: The Electrodynamic Solar System, Exploding Planets and Ancient Wars; Turning the Stream of the Flood: the Origin of Secret Societies and Esoteric Traditions; The Quest to Recover Ancient Mega-Technology; Non-Equilibrium Paleophysics; Monatomic Paleophysics; Frequencies, Vortices and Mass Particles: the Pyramid Power of Dr. Pat Flanagan and Joe Parr; The Topology of the Aether; A Final Physical Effect: "Acoustic" Intensity of Fields; The Pyramid of Crystals; tons more.

292 PAGES. 6x9 PAPERBACK. ILLUSTRATED. BIBLIOGRAPHY. $16.95. CODE: GDES

INVISIBLE RESIDENTS
The Reality of Underwater UFOS
by Ivan T. Sanderson, Foreword by David Hatcher Childress

This book is a groundbreaking contribution to the study of the UFO enigma, originally published over 30 years ago. In this book, Sanderson, a renowned zoologist with a keen interest in the paranormal, puts forward the curious theory that "OINTS"—Other Intelligences—live under the Earth's oceans. This underwater, parallel, civilization may be twice as old as Homo sapiens, he proposes, and may have "developed what we call space flight." Sanderson postulates that the OINTS are behind many UFO sightings as well as the mysterious disappearances of aircraft and ships in the Bermuda Triangle. What better place to have an impenetrable base than deep within the oceans of the planet? Yet, if UFOs, or at least some of them, are coming from beneath our oceans or lakes, does it necessarily mean that there is another civilization besides our own that is responsible? In fact, could it be that since WWII a number of underwater UFO bases have been constructed by the very human governments of our planet? Whatever their source, Sanderson offers here an exhaustive study of USOs (Unidentified Submarine Objects) observed in nearly every part of the world. He presents many well-documented and exciting case studies of these unusual sightings.; more.

298 PAGES. 6x9 PAPERBACK. ILLUSTRATED. BIBLIOGRAPHY. INDEX. $16.95. CODE: INVS

24 hour credit card orders—call: 815-253-6390 fax: 815-253-6300
email: auphq@frontiernet.net   www.adventuresunlimitedpress.com   www.wexclub.com

NEW BOOKS

PERPETUAL MOTION
The History of an Obsession
by Arthur W. J. G. Ord-Hume

Make a machine which gives out more work than the energy you put into it, and you have perpetual motion. The deceptively simple task of making a mechanism which would forever fascinated many an inventor, and a number of famous men and physicists applied themselves to the task. Despite the naivete and blatant trickery of many of the inventors, there are a handful of mechanisms which defy explanation. A vast canvas-covered wheel which turned by itself was erected in the Tower of London. Another wheel, equally surrounded by mystery and intrigue, turned endlessly in Germany. Chapters include: Elementary Physics and Perpetual Motion; Medieval Perpetual Motion; Self-moving Wheels and Overbalancing Weights; Lodestones, Electro-Magnetism and Steam; Capillary Attraction and Spongewheels; Cox's Perpetual Motion; Keely and his Amazing Motor; Odd Ideas about Vaporization and Liquefaction; The Astonishing Case of the Garabed Project; Ever-Ringing Bells and Radium Perpetual Motion; Perpetual Motion Inventors Barred from the US Patent Office; Rolling Ball Clocks; Perpetual Lamps; The Perpetuity of the Perpetual Motion Inventor; more.
260 PAGES. 6x9 PAPERBACK. ILLUSTRATED. BIBLIOGRAPHY. INDEX. $20.00. CODE: PPM

MIND CONTROL AND UFOS
Casebook on Alternative 3
by Jim Keith

Drawing on his diverse research and a wide variety of sources, Jim Keith delves into the bizarre story behind *Alternative 3*, including mind control programs, underground bases not only on the Earth but also on the Moon and Mars, the real origin of the UFO problem, the mysterious deaths of Marconi Electronics employees in Britain during the 1980s, top scientists around the world the secret government space bases, the Russian-American superpower arms race of the 50s, 60s and 70s as a massive hoax, and other startling arenas. Chapters include: Secret Societies and *Die Neuordning*; The Fourth Reich; UFOs and the Space Program; Government UFOs; Hot Jobs and Crop Circles; Missing Scientists and LGIBs; Ice Picks, Electrodes and LSD; Electronic Wars; Batch Consignments; The Depopulation Bomb; Veins and Tributaries; Lunar Base Alpha One; Disinfo; Other Alternatives; Noah's Ark II; *Das Marsprojekt*; more.
248 PAGES. 6x9 PAPERBACK. ILLUSTRATED. BIBLIOGRAPHY. $14.95. CODE: MCUF

SECRETS OF THE HOLY LANCE
The Spear of Destiny in History & Legend
by Jerry E. Smith and George Piccard

As Jesus Christ hung on the cross a Roman centurion pierced the Savior's side with his spear. A legend has arisen that "whosoever possesses this Holy Lance and understands the powers it serves, holds in his hand the destiny of the world for good or evil." *Secrets of the Holy Lance* traces the Spear from its possession by Constantine, Rome's first Christian Caesar, to Charlemagne's claim that with it he ruled the Holy Roman Empire by Divine Right, and on through two thousand years of kings and emperors, until it came within Hitler's grasp—and beyond! Did it rest for a while in Antarctic ice? Is it now hidden in Europe, awaiting the next person to claim its awesome power? Neither debunking nor worshiping, *Secrets of the Holy Lance* seeks to pierce the veil of myth and mystery around the Spear. Mere belief that it was infused with magic by virtue of its shedding the Savior's blood has made men kings. But what if it's more? What are "the powers it serves"?
312 PAGES. 6x9 PAPERBACK. ILLUSTRATED. BIBLIOGRAPHY. $16.95. CODE: SOHL

REICH OF THE BLACK SUN
Nazi Secret Weapons and the Cold War Allied Legend
by Joseph P. Farrell

Why were the Allies worried about an atom bomb attack by the Germans in 1944? Why did the Soviets threaten to use poison gas against the Germans? Why did Hitler in 1945 insist that holding Prague could win the war for the Third Reich? Why did US General George Patton's Third Army race for the Skoda works at Pilsen in Czechoslovakia instead of Berlin? Why did the US Army not test the uranium atom bomb it dropped on Hiroshima? Why did the Luftwaffe fly a non-stop round trip mission to within twenty miles of New York City in 1944? *Reich of the Black Sun* takes the reader on a scientific-historical journey in order to answer these questions. Arguing that Nazi Germany actually won the race for the atom bomb in late 1944, *Reich of the Black Sun* then goes on to explore the even more secretive research the Nazis were conducting into the occult, alternative physics and new energy sources. The book concludes with a fresh look at the "Nazi Legend" of the UFO mystery by examining the Roswell Majestic-12 documents and the Kecksburg crash in the light of parallels with some of the super-secret black projects being run by the SS. *Reich of the Black Sun* is must-reading for the researcher interested in alternative history, science, or UFOs!
352 PAGES. 6x9 PAPERBACK. ILLUSTRATED. BIBLIOGRAPHY. $16.95. CODE: ROBS

UFOS, PSI AND SPIRITUAL EVOLUTION
A Journey through the Evolution of Interstellar Travel
by Christopher Humphries, Ph.D.

The modern era of UFOs began in May, 1947, one year and eight months after Hiroshima. This is no coincidence, and suggests there are beings in the universe with the ability to jump hundreds of light years in an instant. That is teleportation, a power of the mind. If it weren't for levitation and teleportation, star travel would not be possible at all, since physics rules out star travel by technology. So if we want to go to the stars, it is the mind and spirit we must study, not technology. The mind must be a dark matter object, since it is invisible and intangible and can freely pass through solid objects. A disembodied mind can see the de Broglie vibrations (the basis of quantum mechanics) radiated by both dark and ordinary matter during near-death or out-of-body experiences. Levitation requires warping the geodesics of space-time. The latest theory in physics is String Theory, which requires six extra spatial dimensions. The mind warps those higher geodesics to produce teleportation. We are a primitive and violent species. Our universities lack any sciences of mind, spirit or civilization. If we want to go to the stars, the first thing we must do is "grow up." That is the real Journey.
274 PAGES. 6x9 PAPERBACK. ILLUSTRATED. REFERENCES. $16.95. CODE: UPSE

PROFESSOR WEXLER—WORLD EXPLORER
The Wacky Adventures of the World's Greatest Explorer
by Charles Berlin

From the pages of *World Explorer* magazine comes this zany, wacky compilation of cartoons, pulp-era parodies, and comics featuring the never-ending escapades of the intrepid Professor Wexler—a bespectacled, unshaven, unabashed adventurer—into the fringes of the unknown and weird. It includes all of the original cartoons, plus a new feature-length comic of the Professor, and an introduction by *World Explorer* editor and Lost Cities author David Hatcher Childress. With a pipe clenched in his teeth, the ever-resilient professor encounters everything from Bigfoot, UFOs, and the Loch Ness Monster to the dangerous jungles, deserts and denizens of the remote parts of the world. Professor Wexler is a Doc Savage-Indiana Jones character who lives on the edge of life, and one never knows what sort of predicament he will be in next.
126 PAGES. 8x11 PAPERBACK. ILLUSTRATED IN COLOR. $12.00. CODE: PWWE

CONSPIRACY & HISTORY

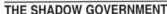

SAUCERS OF THE ILLUMINATI
by Jim Keith, Foreword by Kenn Thomas
Seeking the truth behind stories of alien invasion, secret underground bases, and the secret plans of the New World Order, *Saucers of the Illuminati* offers ground breaking research, uncovering clues to the nature of UFOs and to forces even more sinister: the secret cabal behind planetary control! Includes mind control, saucer abductions, the MJ-12 documents, cattle mutilations, government anti-gravity testing, the Sirius Connection, science fiction author Philip K. Dick and his efforts to expose the Illuminati, plus more from veteran conspiracy and UFO author Keith. Conspiracy expert Keith's final book on UFOs and the highly secret group that manufactures them and uses them for their own purposes: the control and manipulation of the population of planet Earth.
148 PAGES. 6x9 PAPERBACK. ILLUSTRATED. $12.95. CODE: SOIL

THE SHADOW GOVERNMENT
9-11 and State Terror
by Len Bracken, introduction by Kenn Thomas
Bracken presents the alarming yet convincing theory that nation-states engage in or allow terror to be visited upon their citizens. It is not just liberation movements and radical groups that deploy terroristic tactics for offensive ends. States use terror defensively to directly intimidate their citizens and to indirectly attack themselves or harm their citizens under a false flag. Their motives? To provide pretexts for war or for increased police powers or both. This stratagem of indirectly using terrorism has been executed by statesmen in various ways but tends to involve the pretense of blind eyes, misdirection, and cover-ups that give statesmen plausible deniability. Lusitiania, Pearl Harbor, October Surprise, the first World Trade Center bombing, the Oklahoma City bombing and other well-known incidents suggest that terrorism is often and successfully used by states in an indirectly defensive way to take the offensive against enemies at home and abroad. Was 9-11 such an indirect defensive attack?
288 PAGES. 6x9 PAPERBACK. ILLUSTRATED. $16.00. CODE: SGOV

ARKTOS
The Myth of the Pole in Science, Symbolism, and Nazi Survival
by Joscelyn Godwin
A scholarly treatment of catastrophes, ancient myths and the Nazi Occult beliefs. Explored are the many tales of an ancient race said to have lived in the Arctic regions, such as Thule and Hyperborea. Progressing onward, the book looks at modern polar legends including the survival of Hitler, German bases in Antarctica, UFOs, the hollow earth, Agartha and Shambala, more.
220 PAGES. 6x9 PAPERBACK. ILLUSTRATED. $16.95. CODE: ARK

THE LUCID VIEW
Investigations in Occultism, Ufology & Paranoid Awareness
by Aeolus Kephas
An unorthodox analysis of conspiracy theory, ufology, extraterrestrialism and occultism. *The Lucid View* takes us on an impartial journey through secret history, including the Gnostics and Templars; Crowley and Hitler's occult alliance; the sorcery wars of Freemasonry and the Illuminati; "Alternative Three" covert space colonization; the JFK assassination; the Manson murders; Jonestown and 9/11. Also delves into UFOs and alien abductions, their relations to mind control technology and sorcery practices, with reference to inorganic beings and Kundalini energy. The book offers a balanced overview on religious, magical and paranoid beliefs pertaining to the 21st century, and their social, psychological, and spiritual implications for humanity, the leading game player in the grand mythic drama of Armageddon.
298 PAGES. 6x9 PAPERBACK. ILLUSTRATED. $16.95. CODE: LVEW

POPULAR PARANOIA
The Best of Steamshovel Press
edited by Kenn Thomas
The anthology exposes the biologocal warfare origins of AIDS; the Nazi/Nation of Islam link; the cult of Elizabeth Clare Prophet; the Oklahoma City bombing writings of the late Jim Keith, as well as an article on Keith's own strange death; the conspiratorial world of John Judge; Marion Pettie and the shadowy Finders group in Washington, DC; demonic iconography; the death of Princess Diana, its connection to the Octopus and the Saudi aerospace contracts; spies among the Rajneeshis; scholarship on the historic Illuminati; and many other parapolitical topics. The book also includes the Steamshovel's last-ever interviews with the great Beat writers Allen Ginsberg and William S. Burroughs, and neuronaut Timothy Leary, and new views of the master Beat, Neal Cassady and Jack Kerouac's science fiction.
308 PAGES. 8x10 PAPERBACK. ILLUSTRATED. $19.95. CODE: POPA

DARK MOON
Apollo and the Whistleblowers
by Mary Bennett and David Percy
•Did you know a second craft was going to the Moon at the same time as Apollo 11?
•Do you know there are serious discrepancies in the account of the Apollo 13 'accident'?
•Did you know that 'live' color TV from the Moon was not actually live at all?
•Did you know that the Lunar Surface Camera had no viewfinder?
•Do you know that lighting was used in the Apollo photographs—yet no lighting equipment was taken to the Moon? All these questions, and more, are discussed in great detail by British researchers Bennett and Percy in *Dark Moon* (nearly 600 pages) on the possible faking of the Apollo Moon missions. Bennett and Percy delve into every possible aspect of this beguiling theory, one that rocks the very foundation of our beliefs concerning NASA and the space program. Tons of NASA photos analyzed for possible deceptions.
568 PAGES. 6x9 PAPERBACK. ILLUSTRATED. BIBLIOGRAPHY. INDEX. $25.00. CODE: DMO

24 hour credit card orders--call: 815-253-6390 fax: 815-253-6300
email: auphq@frontiernet.net   www.adventuresunlimitedpress.com   www.wexclub.com

CONSPIRACY & HISTORY

MIND CONTROL, WORLD CONTROL
by Jim Keith
Veteran author and investigator Jim Keith uncovers a surprising amount of information on the technology, experimentation and implementation of mind control. Various chapters in this shocking book are on early CIA experiments such as Project Artichoke and Project R.H.I.C.-EDOM, the methodology and technology of implants, mind control assassins and couriers, various famous Mind Control victims such as Sirhan Sirhan and Candy Jones. Also featured in this book are chapters on how mind control technology may be linked to some UFO activity and "UFO abductions."
256 PAGES. 6x9 PAPERBACK. ILLUSTRATED. FOOTNOTES. $14.95. CODE: MCWC

MASS CONTROL
Engineering Human Consciousness
by Jim Keith
Conspiracy expert Keith's final book on mind control, Project Monarch, and mass manipulation presents chilling evidence that we are indeed spinning a Matrix. Keith describes the New Man, where conception of reality is a dance of electronic images fired into his forebrain, a gossamer construction of his masters, designed so that he will not—under any circumstances—perceive the actual. His happiness is delivered to him through a tube or an electronic connection. His God lurks behind an electronic curtain; when the curtain is pulled away we find the CIA sorcerer, the media manipulatorÖ Chapters on the CIA, Tavistock, Jolly West and the Violence Center, Guerrilla Mindwar, Brice Taylor, other recent "victims," more.
256 PAGES. 6x9 PAPERBACK. ILLUSTRATED. INDEX. $16.95. CODE: MASC

LIQUID CONSPIRACY
JFK, LSD, the CIA, Area 51 & UFOs
by George Piccard
Underground author George Piccard on the politics of LSD, mind control, and Kennedy's involvement with Area 51 and UFOs. Reveals JFK's LSD experiences with Mary Pinchot-Meyer. The plot thickens with an ever expanding web of CIA involvement, from underground bases with UFOs seen by JFK and Marilyn Monroe (among others) to a vaster conspiracy that affects every government agency from NASA to the Justice Department. This may have been the reason that Marilyn Monroe and actress-columnist Dorothy Kilgallen were both murdered. Focusing on the bizarre side of history, *Liquid Conspiracy* takes the reader on a psychedelic tour de force. This is your government on drugs!
264 PAGES. 6x9 PAPERBACK. ILLUSTRATED. $14.95. CODE: LIQC

INSIDE THE GEMSTONE FILE
Howard Hughes, Onassis & JFK
by Kenn Thomas & David Hatcher Childress

Steamshovel Press editor Thomas takes on the Gemstone File in this run-up and run-down of the most famous underground document ever circulated. Photocopied and distributed for over 20 years, the Gemstone File is the story of Bruce Roberts, the inventor of the synthetic ruby widely used in laser technology today, and his relationship with the Howard Hughes Company and ultimately with Aristotle Onassis, the Mafia, and the CIA. Hughes kidnapped and held a drugged-up prisoner for 10 years; Onassis and his role in the Kennedy Assassination; how the Mafia ran corporate America in the 1960s; the death of Onassis' son in the crash of a small private plane in Greece; Onassis as Ian Fleming's archvillain Ernst Stavro Blofeld; more.
320 PAGES. 6x9 PAPERBACK. ILLUSTRATED. $16.00. CODE: IGF

NASA, NAZIS & JFK:
The Torbitt Document & the JFK Assassination
introduction by Kenn Thomas
This book emphasizes the links between "Operation Paper Clip" Nazi scientists working for NASA, the assassination of JFK, and the secret Nevada air base Area 51. The Torbitt Document also talks about the roles played in the assassination by Division Five of the FBI, the Defense Industrial Security Command (DISC), the Las Vegas mob, and the shadow corporate entities Permindex and Centro-Mondiale Commerciale. The Torbitt Document claims that the same players planned the 1962 assassination attempt on Charles de Gaul, who ultimately pulled out of NATO because he traced the "Assassination Cabal" to Permindex in Switzerland and to NATO headquarters in Brussels. The Torbitt Document paints a dark picture of NASA, the military industrial complex, and the connections to Mercury, Nevada which headquarters the "secret space program."
258 PAGES. 5x8. PAPERBACK. ILLUSTRATED. $16.00. CODE: NNJ

MIND CONTROL, OSWALD & JFK:
Were We Controlled?
introduction by Kenn Thomas
Steamshovel Press editor Kenn Thomas examines the little-known book *Were We Controlled?*, first published in 1968. The book's author, the mysterious Lincoln Lawrence, maintained that Lee Harvey Oswald was a special agent who was a mind control subject, having received an implant in 1960 at a Russian hospital. Thomas examines the evidence for implant technology and the role it could have played in the Kennedy Assassination. Thomas also looks at the mind control aspects of the RFK assassination and details the history of implant technology. Looks at the case that the reporter Damon Runyon, Jr. was murdered because of this book.
256 PAGES. 6x9 PAPERBACK. ILLUSTRATED. NOTES. $16.00. CODE: MCOJ

24 hour credit card orders—call: 815-253-6390 fax: 815-253-6300
email: auphq@frontiernet.net   www.adventuresunlimitedpress.com   www.wexclub.com

NOSTRADAMUS AND THE LOST TEMPLAR LEGACY
by Rudy Cambier

Rudy Cambier's decade-long research and analysis of the verses of Nostradamus' "prophecies" has shown that the language of those verses does not belong in the 16th Century, nor in Nostradamus' region of Provence. The language spoken in the verses belongs to the medieval times of the 14th Century, and the Belgian borders. The documents known as Nostradamus' prophecies were not written ca. 1550 by the French "visionary" Michel de Nostradame. Instead, they were composed between 1323 and 1328 by a Cistercian monk, Yves de Lessines, prior of the abbey of Cambron, on the border between France and Belgium. According to the author, these documents reveal the location of a Templar treasure. This key allowed Cambier to translate the "prophecies." But rather than being confronted with a series of cataclysms and revelations of future events, Cambier discovered a possibly even more stunning secret. Yves de Lessines had waited for many years for someone called "l'attendu," the expected one. This person was supposed to come to collect the safeguarded treasures of the Knights Templar, an organization suppressed in 1307. But no-one came. Hence, the prior decided to impart the whereabouts and nature of the treasure in a most cryptic manner in verses.

204 PAGES. 6x9 PAPERBACK. ILLUSTRATED. BIBLIOGRAPHY. $17.95. CODE: NLTL

THE FREE-ENERGY DEVICE HANDBOOK
A Compilation of Patents and Reports
by David Hatcher Childress

A large-format compilation of various patents, papers, descriptions and diagrams concerning free-energy devices and systems. *The Free-Energy Device Handbook* is a visual tool for experimenters and researchers into magnetic motors and other "over-unity" devices. With chapters on the Adams Motor, the Hans Coler Generator, cold fusion, superconductors, "N" machines, space-energy generators, Nikola Tesla, T. Townsend Brown, and the latest in free-energy devices. Packed with photos, technical diagrams, patents and fascinating information, this book belongs on every science shelf. With energy and profit being a major political reason for fighting various wars, free-energy devices, if ever allowed to be mass distributed to consumers, could change the world! Get your copy now before the Department of Energy bans this book!

292 PAGES. 8x10 PAPERBACK. ILLUSTRATED. BIBLIOGRAPHY. $16.95. CODE: FEH

THE ANTI-GRAVITY HANDBOOK
edited by David Hatcher Childress, with Nikola Tesla, T.B. Paulicki, Bruce Cathie, Albert Einstein and others

The new expanded compilation of material on Anti-Gravity, Free Energy, Flying Saucer Propulsion, UFOs, Suppressed Technology, NASA Cover-ups and more. Highly illustrated with patents, technical illustrations and photos. This revised and expanded edition has more material, including photos of Area 51, Nevada, the government's secret testing facility. This classic on weird science is back in a 90s format!

230 PAGES. 7x10 PAPERBACK. BIBLIOGRAPHY/INDEX/APPENDIX. HIGHLY ILLUSTRATED. $14.95. CODE: AGH

ANTI–GRAVITY & THE WORLD GRID

Is the earth surrounded by an intricate electromagnetic grid network offering free energy? This compilation of material on ley lines and world power points contains chapters on the geography, mathematics, and light harmonics of the earth grid. Learn the purpose of ley lines and ancient megalithic structures located on the grid. Discover how the grid made the Philadelphia Experiment possible. Explore the Coral Castle and many other mysteries, including acoustic levitation, Tesla Shields and scalar wave weaponry. Browse through the section on anti-gravity patents, and research resources.

274 PAGES. 7x10 PAPERBACK. ILLUSTRATED. $14.95. CODE: AGW

ANTI–GRAVITY & THE UNIFIED FIELD
edited by David Hatcher Childress

Is Einstein's Unified Field Theory the answer to all of our energy problems? Explored in this compilation of material is how gravity, electricity and magnetism manifest from a unified field around us. Why artificial gravity is possible; secrets of UFO propulsion; free energy; Nikola Tesla and anti-gravity airships of the 20s and 30s; flying saucers as superconducting whirls of plasma; anti-mass generators; vortex propulsion; suppressed technology; government cover-ups; gravitational pulse drive; spacecraft & more.

240 PAGES. 7x10 PAPERBACK. ILLUSTRATED. $14.95. CODE: AGU

MAN-MADE UFOS 1944—1994
Fifty Years of Suppression
by Renato Vesco & David Hatcher Childress

A comprehensive look at the early "flying saucer" technology of Nazi Germany and the genesis of man-made UFOs. This book takes us from the work of captured German scientists to escaped battalions of Germans, secret communities in South America and Antarctica to todays state-of-the-art "Dreamland" flying machines. Heavily illustrated, this astonishing book blows the lid off the "government UFO conspiracy" and explains with technical diagrams the technology involved. Examined in detail are secret underground airfields and factories; German secret weapons; "suction" aircraft; the origin of NASA; gyroscopic stabilizers and engines; the secret Marconi aircraft factory in South America; and more. Introduction by W.A. Harbinson, author of the Dell novels GENESIS and REVELATION.

318 PAGES. 6x9 PAPERBACK. ILLUSTRATED. INDEX & FOOTNOTES. $18.95. CODE: MMU

FREE ENERGY SYSTEMS

Leonard G. Cramp

COSMIC MATRIX
Piece for a Jig-Saw, Part Two
by Leonard G. Cramp

Leonard G. Cramp, a British aerospace engineer, wrote his first book *Space Gravity and the Flying Saucer* in 1954. Cosmic Matrix is the long-awaited sequel to his 1966 book *UFOs & Anti-Gravity: Piece for a Jig-Saw.* Cramp has had a long history of examining UFO phenomena and has concluded that UFOs use the highest possible aeronautic science to move in the way they do. Cramp examines anti-gravity effects and theorizes that this super-science used by the craft—described in detail in the book—can lift mankind into a new level of technology, transportation and understanding of the universe. The book takes a close look at gravity control, time travel, and the interlocking web of energy between all planets in our solar system with Leonard's unique technical diagrams. A fantastic voyage into the present and future!
364 PAGES. 6x9 PAPERBACK. ILLUSTRATED. BIBLIOGRAPHY. $16.00. CODE: CMX

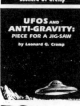

UFOS AND ANTI-GRAVITY
Piece For A Jig-Saw
by Leonard G. Cramp

Leonard G. Cramp's 1966 classic book on flying saucer propulsion and suppressed technology is a highly technical look at the UFO phenomena by a trained scientist. Cramp first introduces the idea of 'anti-gravity' and introduces us to the various theories of gravitation. He then examines the technology necessary to build a flying saucer and examines in great detail the technical aspects of such a craft. Cramp's book is a wealth of material and diagrams on flying saucers, anti-gravity, suppressed technology, G-fields and UFOs. Chapters include Crossroads of Aerodymanics, Aerodynamic Saucers, Limitations of Rocketry, Gravitation and the Ether, Gravitational Spaceships, G-Field Lift Effects, The Bi-Field Theory, VTOL and Hovercraft, Analysis of UFO photos, more.
388 PAGES. 6x9 PAPERBACK. ILLUSTRATED. $16.95. CODE: UAG

THE TIME TRAVEL HANDBOOK
A Manual of Practical Teleportation & Time Travel
edited by David Hatcher Childress

In the tradition of *The Anti-Gravity Handbook* and *The Free-Energy Device Handbook,* science and UFO author David Hatcher Childress takes us into the weird world of time travel and teleportation. Not just a whacked-out look at science fiction, this book is an authoritative chronicling of real-life time travel experiments, teleportation devices and more. *The Time Travel Handbook* takes the reader beyond the government experiments and deep into the uncharted territory of early time travellers such as Nikola Tesla and Guglielmo Marconi and their alleged time travel experiments, as well as the Wilson Brothers of EMI and their connection to the Philadelphia Experiment—the U.S. Navy's forays into invisibility, time travel, and teleportation. Childress looks into the claims of time travelling individuals, and investigates the unusual claim that the pyramids on Mars were built in the future and sent back in time. A highly visual, large format book, with patents, photos and schematics. Be the first on your block to build your own time travel device!
316 PAGES. 7x10 PAPERBACK. ILLUSTRATED. $16.95. CODE: TTH

THE TESLA PAPERS
Nikola Tesla on Free Energy & Wireless Transmission of Power
by Nikola Tesla, edited by David Hatcher Childress

David Hatcher Childress takes us into the incredible world of Nikola Tesla and his amazing inventions. Tesla's rare article "The Problem of Increasing Human Energy with Special Reference to the Harnessing of the Sun's Energy" is included. This lengthy article was originally published in the June 1900 issue of *The Century Illustrated Monthly Magazine* and it was the outline for Tesla's master blueprint for the world. Tesla's fantastic vision of the future, including wireless power, anti-gravity, free energy and highly advanced solar power. Also included are some of the papers, patents and material collected on Tesla at the Colorado Springs Tesla Symposiums, including papers on: •The Secret History of Wireless Transmission •Tesla and the Magnifying Transmitter •Design and Construction of a Half-Wave Tesla Coil •Electrostatics: A Key to Free Energy •Progress in Zero-Point Energy Research •Electromagnetic Energy from Antennas to Atoms •Tesla's Particle Beam Technology •Fundamental Excitatory Modes of the Earth-Ionosphere Cavity
325 PAGES. 8X10 PAPERBACK. ILLUSTRATED. $16.95. CODE: TTP

THE FANTASTIC INVENTIONS OF NIKOLA TESLA
by Nikola Tesla with additional material by David Hatcher Childress

This book is a readable compendium of patents, diagrams, photos and explanations of the many incredible inventions of the originator of the modern era of electrification. In Tesla's own words are such topics as wireless transmission of power, death rays, and radio-controlled airships. In addition, rare material on German bases in Antarctica and South America, and a secret city built at a remote jungle site in South America by one of Tesla's students, Guglielmo Marconi. Marconi's secret group claims to have built flying saucers in the 1940s and to have gone to Mars in the early 1950s! Incredible photos of these Tesla craft are included. The Ancient Atlantean system of broadcasting energy through a grid system of obelisks and pyramids is discussed, and a fascinating concept comes out of one chapter: that Egyptian engineers had to wear protective metal head-shields while in these power plants, hence the Egyptian Pharoah's head covering as well as the Face on Mars! •His plan to transmit free electricity into the atmosphere. •How electrical devices would work using only small antennas. •Why unlimited power could be utilized anywhere on earth. •How radio and radar technology can be used as death-ray weapons in Star Wars.
342 PAGES. 6x9 PAPERBACK. ILLUSTRATED. $16.95. CODE: FINT

24 hour credit card orders—call: 815-253-6390 fax: 815-253-6300
email: auphq@frontiernet.net   www.adventuresunlimitedpress.com   www.wexclub.com

MYSTIC TRAVELLER SERIES

THE MYSTERY OF EASTER ISLAND
by Katherine Routledge
The reprint of Katherine Routledge's classic archaeology book which was first published in London in 1919. The book details her journey by yacht from England to South America, around Patagonia to Chile and on to Easter Island. Routledge explored the amazing island and produced one of the first-ever accounts of the life, history and legends of this strange and remote place. Routledge discusses the statues, pyramid-platforms, Rongo Rongo script, the Bird Cult, the war between the Short Ears and the Long Ears, the secret caves, ancient roads on the island, and more. This rare book serves as a sourcebook on the early discoveries and theories on Easter Island.
432 PAGES. 6X9 PAPERBACK. ILLUSTRATED. $16.95. CODE: MEI

MYSTERY CITIES OF THE MAYA
Exploration and Adventure in Lubaantun & Belize
by Thomas Gann

First published in 1925, *Mystery Cities of the Maya* is a classic in Central American archaeology-adventure. Gann was close friends with Mike Mitchell-Hedges, the British adventurer who discovered the famous crystal skull with his adopted daughter Sammy and Lady Richmond Brown, their benefactress. Gann battles pirates along Belize's coast and goes upriver with Mitchell-Hedges to the site of Lubaantun where they excavate a strange lost city where the crystal skull was discovered. Lubaantun is a unique city in the Mayan world as it is built out of precisely carved blocks of stone without the usual plaster-cement facing. Lubaantun contained several large pyramids partially destroyed by earthquakes and a large amount of artifacts. Gann shared Mitchell-Hedges belief in Atlantis and lost civilizations (pre-Mayan) in Central America and the Caribbean. Lots of good photos, maps and diagrams.
252 PAGES. 6X9 PAPERBACK. ILLUSTRATED. $16.95. CODE: MCOM

IN SECRET TIBET
by Theodore Illion

Reprint of a rare 30s adventure travel book. Illion was a German wayfarer who not only spoke fluent Tibetan, but travelled in disguise as a native through forbidden Tibet when it was off-limits to all outsiders. His incredible adventures make this one of the most exciting travel books ever published. Includes illustrations of Tibetan monks levitating stones by acoustics.
210 PAGES. 6X9 PAPERBACK. ILLUSTRATED. $15.95. CODE: IST

DARKNESS OVER TIBET
by Theodore Illion
In this second reprint of Illion's rare books, the German traveller continues his journey through Tibet and is given directions to a strange underground city. As the original publisher's remarks said, "this is a rare account of an underground city in Tibet by the only Westerner ever to enter it and escape alive! "
210 PAGES. 6X9 PAPERBACK. ILLUSTRATED. $15.95. CODE: DOT

IN SECRET MONGOLIA
by Henning Haslund

First published by Kegan Paul of London in 1934, Haslund takes us into the barely known world of Mongolia of 1921, a land of god-kings, bandits, vast mountain wilderness and a Russian army running amok. Starting in Peking, Haslund journeys to Mongolia as part of the Krebs Expedition—a mission to establish a Danish butter farm in a remote corner of northern Mongolia. Along the way, he smuggles guns and nitroglycerin, is thrown into a prison by the new Communist regime, battles the Robber Princess and more. With Haslund we meet the "Mad Baron" Ungern-Sternberg and his renegade Russian army, the many characters of Urga's fledgling foreign community, and the last god-king of Mongolia, Seng Chen Gegen, the fifth reincarnation of the Tiger god and the "ruler of all Torguts." Aside from the esoteric and mystical material, there is plenty of just plain adventure: Haslund encounters a Mongolian werewolf; is ambushed along the trail; escapes from prison and fights terrifying blizzards; more.
374 PAGES. 6X9 PAPERBACK. ILLUSTRATED. BIB. & INDEX. $16.95. CODE: ISM

MEN & GODS IN MONGOLIA
by Henning Haslund

First published in 1935 by Kegan Paul of London, Haslund takes us to the lost city of Karakota in the Gobi desert. We meet the Bodgo Gegen, a god-king in Mongolia similar to the Dalai Lama of Tibet. We meet Dambin Jansang, the dreaded warlord of the "Black Gobi." There is even material in this incredible book on the Hi-mori, an "airhorse" that flies through the sky (similar to a Vimana) and carries with it the sacred stone of Chintamani. Aside from the esoteric and mystical material, there is plenty of just plain adventure: Haslund and companions journey across the Gobi desert by camel caravan; are kidnapped and held for ransom; witness initiation into Shamanic societies; meet reincarnated warlords; and experience the violent birth of "modern" Mongolia.
358 PAGES. 6X9 PAPERBACK. ILLUSTRATED. INDEX. $15.95. CODE: MGM

ATLANTIS STUDIES

MAPS OF THE ANCIENT SEA KINGS
Evidence of Advanced Civilization in the Ice Age
by Charles H. Hapgood
Charles Hapgood's classic 1966 book on ancient maps produces concrete evidence of an advanced world-wide civilization existing many thousands of years before ancient Egypt. He has found the evidence in the Piri Reis Map that shows Antarctica, the Hadji Ahmed map, the Oronteus Finaeus and other amazing maps. Hapgood concluded that these maps were made from more ancient maps from the various ancient archives around the world, now lost. Not only were these unknown people more advanced in mapmaking than any people prior to the 18th century, it appears they mapped all the continents. The Americas were mapped thousands of years before Columbus. Antarctica was mapped when its coasts were free of ice.
316 PAGES. 7X10 PAPERBACK. ILLUSTRATED. BIB. & INDEX. $19.95. CODE: MASK

PATH OF THE POLE
Cataclysmic Pole Shift Geology
by Charles Hapgood
Maps of the Ancient Sea Kings author Hapgood's classic book *Path of the Pole* is back in print! Hapgood researched Antarctica, ancient maps and the geological record to conclude that the Earth's crust has slipped in the inner core many times in the past, changing the position of the pole. *Path of the Pole* discusses the various "pole shifts" in Earth's past, giving evidence for each one, and moves on to possible future pole shifts. Packed with illustrations, this is the sourcebook for many other books on cataclysms and pole shifts.
356 PAGES. 6X9 PAPERBACK. ILLUSTRATED. $16.95. CODE: POP.

RIDDLE OF THE PACIFIC
by John Macmillan Brown

Charles Hapgood
Author of
Maps of the Ancient Sea Kings

THE RIDDLE OF THE PACIFIC

JOHN MACMILLAN BROWN

This rare 1924 book is back in print!

Oxford scholar Brown's classic work on lost civilizations of the Pacific is now back in print! John Macmillan Brown was an historian and New Zealand's premier scientist when he wrote about the origins of the Maoris. After many years of travel thoughout the Pacific studying the people and customs of the south seas islands, he wrote *Riddle of the Pacific* in 1924. The book is packed with rare turn-of-the-century illustrations. Don't miss Brown's classic study of Easter Island, ancient scripts, megalithic roads and cities, more. Brown was an early believer in a lost continent in the Pacific.
460 PAGES. 6X9 PAPERBACK. ILLUSTRATED. $16.95. CODE: ROP

ATLANTIS IN AMERICA
Ancient World
Ivar Zapp and
George Erikson

ATLANTIS IN AMERICA
Navigators of the Ancient World
by Ivar Zapp and George Erikson
This book is an intensive examination of the archeological sites of the Americas, an examination that reveals civilization has existed here for tens of thousands of years. Zapp is an expert on the enigmatic giant stone spheres of Costa Rica, and maintains that they were sighting stones similar to those found throughout the Pacific as well as in Egypt and the Middle East. They were used to teach star-paths and sea navigation to the world-wide navigators of the ancient world. While the Mediterranean and European regions "forgot" world-wide navigation and fought wars, the Mesoamericans of diverse races were building vast interconnected cities without walls. This Golden Age of ancient America was merely a myth of suppressed history—until now. Profusely illustrated, chapters are on Navigators of the Ancient World; Pyramids & Megaliths: Older Than You Think; Ancient Ports and Colonies; Cataclysms of the Past; Atlantis: From Myth to Reality; The Serpent and the Cross: The Loss of the City States; Calendars and Star Temples; and more.
360 PAGES. 6X9 PAPERBACK. ILLUSTRATED. BIBLIO.. & IX. $17.95. CODE: AIA

FAR-OUT ADVENTURES   *REVISED EDITION*
The Best of World Explorer Magazine
This is a compilation of the first nine issues of *World Explorer* in a large-format paperback. Authors include: David Hatcher Childress, Joseph Jochmans, John Major Jenkins, Deanna Emerson, Katherine Routledge, Alexander Horvat, Greg Deyermenjian, Dr. Marc Miller, and others. Articles in this book include Smithsonian Gate, Dinosaur Hunting in the Congo, Secret Writings of the Incas, On the Trail of the Yeti, Secrets of the Sphinx, Living Pterodactyls, Quest for Atlantis, What Happened to the Great Library of Alexandria?, In Search of Seamonsters, Egyptians in the Pacific, Lost Megaliths of Guatemala, the Mystery of Easter Island, Comacalco: Mayan City of Mystery, Professor Wexler and plenty more.
580 PAGES. 8X11 PAPERBACK. ILLUSTRATED. REVISED EDITION. $25.00. CODE: FOA

RETURN OF THE SERPENTS OF WISDOM
by Mark Amaru Pinkham
According to ancient records, the patriarchs and founders of the early civilizations in Egypt, India, China, Peru, Mesopotamia, Britain, and the Americas were the Serpents of Wisdom—spiritual masters associated with the serpent—who arrived in these lands after abandoning their beloved homelands and crossing great seas. While bearing names denoting snake or dragon (such as Naga, Lung, Djedhi, Amaru, Quetzalcoatl, Adder, etc.), these Serpents of Wisdom oversaw the construction of magnificent civilizations within which they and their descendants served as the priest kings and as the enlightened heads of mystery school traditions. *The Return of the Serpents of Wisdom* recounts the history of these "Serpents"—where they came from, why they came, the secret wisdom they disseminated, and why they are returning now.
400 PAGES. 6X9 PAPERBACK. ILLUSTRATED. REFERENCES. $16.95. CODE: RSW

24 hour credit card orders—call: 815-253-6390 fax: 815-253-6300
email: auphq@frontiernet.net   www.adventuresunlimitedpress.com   www.wexclub.com